Cross-curricular Approaches to Teaching and Learning

Cross-curricular Approaches to Teaching and Learning

edited by

Chris Rowley and Hilary Cooper

Los Angeles | London | New Delhi
Singapore | Washington DC

First published 2009

SAGE Publications Ltd
1 Oliver's Yard
55 City Road
London EC1Y 1SP

SAGE Publications Inc.
2455 Teller Road
Thousand Oaks, California 91320

SAGE Publications India Pvt Ltd
B 1/I 1 Mohan Cooperative Industrial Area
Mathura Road
New Delhi 110 044

SAGE Publications Asia-Pacific Pte Ltd
33 Pekin Street #02-01
Far East Square
Singapore 048763

Library of Congress Control Number 2008938674

British Library Cataloguing in Publication data

A catalogue record for this book is available from the British Library

ISBN 978-1-84787-594-5
ISBN 978-1-84787-595-2 (pbk)

Typeset by C&M Digitals (P) Ltd, Chennai, India
Printed in India at Replika Press Pvt Ltd
Printed on paper from sustainable resources

Contents

Foreword

Recent and ongoing developments in the Qualifications and Curriculum Authority (QCA) Futures programme suggest that we are entering an exciting period in which opportunities to place subjects alongside processes, values, social justice and broader areas of learning make this book timely in exploring existing work that is taking place in schools now.

All the contributors to this book are committed to the development of a more integrated and coherent primary curriculum which makes links between different subjects. They recognize the achievements of the National Curriculum in identifying the concepts and core questions which lie at the heart of each subject and of progression in the skills associated with those questions. They wish to explore ways of taking the curriculum beyond simply linking subjects under a theme, although there are many ways in which this can be done. They are also exploring ways of creating a curriculum which has values education at the heart, not just of classroom organization, relationships and ethos, but also within the core of each subject. For reasons which are explained in Chapter 1, planning for each case study starts with a humanities subject, history or geography – or both – linked to other subjects.

In each example we focus on types of enquiry in which values are embedded in the enquiry itself and not seen as an 'add on'. Values development is part of the teaching of both history and geography, it is a central part of the subjects which cannot be ignored and offers great opportunities to enrich the curriculum.

The case studies, covering Reception to Year 6, are a way of not just explaining and justifying this approach but of sharing with readers, reflecting upon and evaluating what happened when it was put into practice. Most took place over a short period of time in which teachers and teacher trainers worked together to plan and implement them in real classrooms.

It is hoped that these case studies will serve as a stimulation – even an inspiration – for modifying in the context of other school environments. It may be that after the initial integrated unit the contributing subjects develop separately and traditionally within the values theme, and that, at certain points during the longer unit, opportunities are found for further integrated work. This would seem to be a manageable, flexible and developmental model.

What we think is most innovative is that the subjects in each case study are truly integrated, not running alongside each other, and this integration is deepened by the overarching theme which permeates the unit of work, which is an aspect of values education.

Finally, we hope that we have taken both a reflective and exploratory approach. We have experienced a great deal of prescription and the notion that 'someone else, out there, knows best'. It is time to return to applying and evaluating our considerable professional expertise. Recognizing that there are always different and perhaps better ways of doing things and thinking about them deeply, and in relation to our very different professional contexts and understanding that we may all do things differently but equally well, is what attracts well-informed, creative, committed and enthusiastic colleagues to our very important and sometimes undervalued profession. Read on!

Contributor biographies

Jennifer (Jen) Ager is a primary school teacher in High Hesket, Cumbria. She graduated from St Martin's College in 2002 with a physical education (PE) specialism, and has since taught in Plymouth and Cumbria, as well as squeezing in a three-year career break travelling the globe. Jennifer has a keen interest in thematic approaches to the curriculum and uses as many opportunities as she can to link topic work through cross-curricular approaches in her class teaching.

Jan Ashbridge is Subject Leader and Senior Lecturer in Early Childhood Education at the University of Cumbria. She has been a Foundation Stage teacher for 12 years and also a senior advisory teacher for the Foundation Stage within Cumbria Local Education Authority (LEA). Jan has been involved in planning and delivering training to students, and early years educators across the north-west of England in all aspects of young children's learning and the skills adults need to support this.

Chris Barlow lectures in primary geography and history at the University of Cumbria. With 18 successful years in primary education, Chris has been a deputy headteacher and has worked as an advisory teacher for Lancashire LEA. Chris is an experienced subject leader, with an interest in the global dimension, creativity and the development of effective cross-curricular approaches to learning.

Andrea Brook is a senior lecturer in Art and Design at the University of Cumbria with particular interest in book arts and art history and she strongly believes that art can stimulate children in all aspects of their schooling. She has taught in primary schools in the UK, Greece and Austria, where she co-ordinated art in the International School of Vienna.

Dr Hilary Cooper graduated in history and taught for many years in London primary schools. Her doctoral research was on young children's thinking in history, undertaken as a practising class teacher. She was a lecturer in education at Goldsmith's College, London University, before becoming Head of Professional Studies in the Education Department of Lancaster University, and subsequently, Professor of History and Pedagogy at the University of Cumbria. She has published widely on the teaching and learning of history.

Donna Hurford, while working as a primary school teacher, Donna sought opportunities to introduce development education into the curriculum. Her school experience and responsibilities for information and communications technology (ICT) co-ordination enabled her to attain a lecturer post in initial teacher education (ITE). Her current teaching role in higher education, at the University of Cumbria, straddles ICT education and education studies, while her core interest remains with what is now called global citizenship. Part of her role is to support colleagues in the education faculty with the introduction and application of global citizenship themes and principles through a broad range of ITE courses. She has recently returned from a Voluntary Service Overseas (VSO) post in the Maldives where she worked as an adviser for the country's Professional Development Unit, a wonderful professional and personal experience which gave her the opportunity to work in partnership with Maldivian colleagues and to experience living in a very different country.

Jo Josephidou has been an early years teacher since 1988. During her career she has worked in both primary and nursery schools across Foundation Stage (FS) and Key Stage I (KS1). Her main areas of interest are early literacy, primary geography, and personal, social and emotional development in young children. She has led on creative curricula in her current role.

Lisa MacGregor has been a primary school teacher for 14 years. She has had experience of teaching children from Nursery to Year 6 in a range of schools. At present she teaches part time in a primary school in Newcastle upon Tyne and lectures part time at the University of Cumbria.

Hugh Moore is a senior lecturer in primary history and early history at the University of Cumbria. He is a trained teacher and museum curator and in a former life ran the museum's education service in Lancaster and in Trowbridge, Wiltshire.

Graham Reeves is Director of Fieldwork Education Services and has been with fieldwork education for 10 years. Graham was formerly head teacher of a large primary school in the UK and has been an inspector for the Office for Standards in Education (Ofsted), a member of the Special Education Needs Tribunal, visiting lecturer at the universities of Greenwich, London and East London and an acting regional officer for the National Union of Teachers. Graham now works with international schools in many countries. He was responsible for the early development of the International Primary Curriculum (IPC) and has provided IPC training to schools in many locations throughout the world.

Chris Rowley is a senior lecturer in environmental and geographical education at the University of Cumbria. He was a member of the committee of the Society to Advance Philosophical Enquiry in Education (SAPERE) from 1997 to 2003. An interest in children's understanding of the environment led him to work with teachers around Morecambe Bay between 2003 and 2004 to co-produce the book *Thinking on The Edge* (Lewis and Rowley, Living Earth, 2004). In 2006 Chris was co-editor of *Geography 3–11* (Fulton).

Martin Skelton is one of the founders of Fieldwork Education. He designed and was Founding Director of the International Primary Curriculum and continues to be closely involved in its development including the recent direction of its Assessment for Learning Programme. Martin also designed the Looking for Learning protocol which is being used by an increasing number of schools in the UK and elsewhere. He is Director of Learning for the WCLS Group of Schools in the USA and Qatar and is currently leading the writing of the social studies curriculum for a country in the Middle East. Martin has worked with thousands of teachers, administrators and schools around the world, and for the past seven years he has been immersed in brain research and its implications for classroom practice.

Sue Temple graduated from Sunderland Polytechnic and specialized in special educational needs with an M.Ed from Newcastle University. She taught in primary schools in the North East for 17 years, teaching from Nursery to Year 6, including special needs responsibilities and acting head of a nursery school. She is currently course leader for primary history at the Carlisle Campus of the University of Cumbria.

Rob Wheatley taught in inner London for 20 years, first at North Westminster Community school and then at Langdon Park School in Tower Hamlets. His subject was Geography but he taught in a humanities faculty throughout his career. He was Head of Humanities at Langdon Park for 12 years. He has written contributions to books on geography and ICT and was the author of a General Certificate of Secondary Education (GCSE) geography textbook. Since 1997 he has worked in teacher training, first at the Urban Learning Foundation and, since 1999, at St Martin's College London base in Tower Hamlets, now part of the University of Cumbria. He teaches ICT and geography and is currently undertaking research in newly qualified teachers' experiences of teaching geography.

1

Cross-curricular learning and the development of values

Chris Rowley and Hilary Cooper

Chapter introduction

Hilary Cooper and Chris Rowley, together with Donna Hurford, of the University of Cumbria link the case studies in this book to the broader questions surrounding the learning of values through cross-curricular work in primary humanities. The discussion of each key area is supported with further material available on the website page for this book: www.sagepub.co.uk/rowleyandcooper

---

Why we have written this book

We decided to take the humanities subjects, history and geography, as the starting point for planning our case studies, because these subjects have people at their centre. They are concerned with decisions that people make now and made in the past, within the circumstances in which they lived. They are concerned with values. And values are supposed to underpin the curriculum. Values are seen as central to the ethos of a school community but often they are learned through relationships established within the classroom to develop mutual respect, and the way the curriculum is organized to promote inclusion. We wanted to see how values education could also be at the centre of the subjects of the curriculum. Could we design values-based enquiries?

Cross-curricular learning

For a discussion on the historical context of cross curricular learning see website material (WM) 1.1.

Our understanding of cross-curricular learning

In this book we broadly follow Dewey (1902) in a belief that there is no benefit in creating a false opposition between 'subjects' and 'child' as a focus for curriculum. We see them as mutually interdependent in an educational sense. Furthermore, like Dewey, we see 'knowing' and 'valuing' as part of a whole, which needs to be infused through our experiences. We deliberately avoid the rather sterile and polarized debate about 'topics' and 'themes', and instead search for examples of robust links between subjects; links which take account of the discrete thinking processes at the heart of different subjects and relate them through children's experiences.

Discussions with teachers at Pennington School in Cumbria as they began the process of moving back into whole-school cross-curricular planning identified a number of reflections which help to clarify the range of reasons that might be used for such a move. Pennington planned its cross-curricular work by starting from the main subject objectives and then identifying themes which would achieve those.

'Many of the children find visualization hard; art often helps visualizing the meanings found in text' (Bryan Singleton, Year 6 teacher). As an example Bryan planned five weeks' work using Tennyson's poem 'The Lady of Shalott' in which art helped keep the children's interest throughout the period. He found that the different ways of seeing the world used by different subjects made the theme more inclusive, enabling children to respond to different types of text. Neil Davies, also a teacher at Pennington, found that the foundation subjects often offered ways into the other subjects and that time was freed up by the cross-curricular planning that made it possible to study subjects in more depth rather than less. His example of using the Egyptians as a history theme led into trigonometry, ICT and language work.

Clearly cross-curricular planning raises real issues for many teachers, particularly in finding a balance between teacher-led perceptions of how subjects link and others' understanding of those links. On the one hand, there has to be individual appraisal and choice based on the teacher's professional judgement; on the other hand, the school itself needs to have whole-school policies that enable long-term tracking and assessment for learning.

Figure 1.1 shows how we have attempted to illustrate a range of approaches to cross-curricular work in which history and geography form the main stimulus. In each case study a different stimulus is used in order to develop an enquiry in which other subjects play an important role in developing the skills and understanding necessary to develop values emerging in the theme.

Chapter	Key Stage	Time Scale	Distinctive aspects of approach to cross-curricular planning	History or geography focus	Other subjects developed
2	Fndn. Stage		Focusing on the *inherent cross-curricular nature* of all Foundation Stage work	Geography	All areas of learning
3	KS 2		A topic linking history and mathematics enables children to address deeply held *values about identity* through a range of activities	History	Mathematics and English
4	Whole school	A week	Using the **local area** as a familiar location with a focus on using art to enable children to see the unfamiliar in their area	Geography and history	Art
5	KS 2	A week	Using a *visit to an unfamiliar location* and the imperative of a final presentation using ICT as the integrating force	Geography	ICT
6	KS 1	A week	Using historical research into an individual who challenges our stereotypes to *drive key questions for different subjects* after a museum sleepover	History	RE, literacy and numeracy
7	KS 2	A week	Focus on developing historical enquiry and *other subjects to explore the possible thoughts and feelings of people in the past*	History and geography; Tudor exploration	D&T, art, science, literacy, geography
8	KS 2	2 years	Long-term and partnership approaches and *developing clarity through revisiting complex concepts* on the environment	Geography and environmental education	Art, D&T and science
9	KS 1	Med. term week projects	*Making connections* between ways of seeing the world as a way of developing 'international mindedness'	Geography and history	Science and art
10	KS 2	Intermittent	*Using dialogue as a way of linking subjects.* Philosophy for children in which good reasoning is celebrated over content leading inevitably to cross-curricular outcomes	Geography	PSHE, citizenship, literacy and global citizenship

Figure 1.1 How the case studies in this book, focusing on history and geography in different contexts, link with other subjects and have values education embedded within them

The humanities at the heart of a value-laden curriculum

The case studies in this book illustrate contexts and strategies for making links between subjects in the primary curriculum in order to make it more integrated and relevant to learners. The case studies are innovative in two ways. They explore ways in which the core values, which are intended to underpin the whole curriculum, can be embedded not just in classroom organization and ethos but also at the heart of subjects. Planning curriculum links within this value-laden curriculum, we take the humanities, (history or geography or both), as the starting point.

Pike and Selby (2000) identified four dimensions to the curriculum, building on their previous work going back to 1987. They spoke of the need for four components to any future curriculum:

1 a spatial dimension
2 a temporal dimension
3 an issues dimension
4 a process dimension.

Dimensions 1 to 3 clearly relate closely to the knowledge embedded in history and geography. They defined the fourth dimension as the 'inner dimension'. Hicks (2007) has further developed this dimension and defined it as including values. In this book we argue that the process dimension is fundamentally associated with the processes of enquiry that are embedded in the humanities and which bring a number of special characteristics to the process of learning (see, for example, Rowley, 2006). Values is part of that enquiry process and in this book each chapter identifies a variety of types of enquiry.

It is gratifying to see the new curriculum emerging with some of these principles clearly at its heart. (QCA Futures programme weblink (WL) 1.1)

Why start with history and geography?

First, history and geography are essentially concerned with people, with humanity. They are concerned with the reasons people make decisions about how to live, both in their personal lives and in the ways in which societies are organized, within the constraints of different and changing times and places. These decisions involve making choices, which involve ethical considerations. Second, history and geography are 'umbrella subjects'. They encompass all aspects of societies: art and music, literature and beliefs. These subjects therefore link naturally with humanities-based topics. Third, literacy skills, often seen as the starting point for planning curriculum links, were intended in the National Literacy Framework to be applied across the curriculum and developed in coherent contexts.

History and geography, of course, are not alone in offering opportunities to develop values (see WM 1.2), but we believe that they often offer the best starting point, the context and wonderful, practical stimulation for enquires in which values can be explored.

Aim of the case studies

With the exception of one case study, which runs over two years, the case studies are short, taking place over between one and two weeks. This is because we were exploring possibilities in, we hope, creative ways. Before committing to a particular way of organizing the curriculum for a whole school and over a long period of time, it is important to try out ideas on a small scale and evaluate them. Readers may, therefore, want to modify some of the ideas in this book as a starting point. This may, for example, be at the beginning of a unit of work after which the contributing subjects are developed separately, but possibly still within the value-laden theme, perhaps building in some further sessions in which the subjects are integrated within the theme.

The connection between cross-curricular learning and values education

What do we mean by 'values'?

The traditional approach to moral development was to teach virtues through example and reward but this assumed a consensus which did not exist and teachers often imposed their own societal, personal and cultural beliefs. So, in looking for consensus, perhaps we should go back to the Universal Declaration of Human Rights in 1948: 'Education shall be directed to the full development of the human personality and to the strengthening of respect for human rights and fundamental freedoms' (Article 2, paragraph 2).

It could be argued that schools have always seen their role as communicating, respect for the dignity and views of others and values such as tolerance but, given our present fragmented and diverse society, increasingly rapid changes and the global dimension, there have been recent, urgent attempts to define what exactly are the values commonly agreed across British society. The National Forum for Values in Education and the Community identified values which, whether seen as resulting from human conscience or as given (1997: 147–9), have the authority of consensus. These core values were:

- valuing ourselves as unique human beings, capable of spiritual, moral, intellectual and physical growth (so we should actively engage with decision making and problem solving at the heart of subjects)
- valuing relationships as a fulfilment of ourselves, of others and for the good of the community (so involvement in the locality and community is part of education)
- valuing society, respecting truth, justice, human rights, the rule of law, collective efforts for the common good and valuing families, of whatever kind, as sources of love and care for others (how has respect for justice, human rights and the rule of law developed in society?)
- valuing environment, accepting responsibility to maintain a sustainable environment, understand our place in nature and responsibilities for other species (so we need to understand and take some responsibility for environmental problems).

Figure 1.2 shows how these link to the case studies in this book.

History and geography encompass decisions to be made now and understanding the reasons for those made in the past. This lies at the core of the humanities and we argue that this understanding is central to the development of these core values and is also closely associated with the types of enquiry used in the classroom. (WL 1.2 and 1.3)

Values in the National Curriculum

The National Curriculum handbook (DfEE/QCA, 1999: 10–13; 19–21) attempts to identify ways in which schools can reflect and promote these values by providing opportunities to learn and achieve, making learning enjoyable, building on the strengths, interests and experiences of all pupils, promoting enquiring minds and the capacity to think rationally and creatively, contributing to pupils' sense of identity through understanding of the spiritual, moral, social and cultural heritages of diverse societies, in the local, national and global dimensions of their lives, and generally to enable pupils to make a difference for the better.

Through the spiritual, moral, social and cultural dimensions of education schools should enable pupils to develop principles for distinguishing right from wrong, appreciate their own and different beliefs and cultures, challenge discrimination and stereotyping, understand and respect the environments they live in, secure their commitment to sustainable development at a personal, national, local and

Chapter	Type of enquiry, stimulus and process	Some of the values developed in the case study
2	Enquiry through play	Ourselves and our relationships
3	Enquiry through comparison and reflection	Our identity and society
4	Enquiry stimulated by the way we represent a place though the arts	Our community
5	Enquiry stimulated by a visit	Our community and environment
6	Enquiry stimulated by a dilemma	Truth, justice, family and the common good
7	Enquiry stimulated by different ways of seeing	Truth and justice
8	Enquiry stimulated by a focus on conceptual understanding	Environment
9	Enquiry stimulated by themes which focus on connections	Social justice
10	Enquiry stimulated by questioning and whole-class dialogue	Social justice

Figure 1.2   The types of enquiry used in this book and the connection with values developed

Note: Many of the approaches to enquiry and values in Figure 1.2 are developed throughout the book. This figure is an attempt to identify the main focus of each chapter.

global level and promote self-esteem, emotional well-being, respect for others and work with others for the common good.

There have been initiatives which have attempted to translate these grandiose principles into practical contexts. The five intended outcomes of the *Every Child Matters and Youth Matters* agenda (QCA, 2005a) reflect the aims of the School Curriculum: to be healthy, stay safe, enjoy and achieve, engage in decision-making and positive relationships and to 'achieve economic well-being'. The *Excellence and Enjoyment* programme (DfEE/QCA, 2003) attempts a broader and more practical approach to realizing the aims, through school ethos and innovation, excellent teaching, a focus on individual learning, partnership beyond the classroom and working collaboratively in order to realize the vision. *The Futures Programme: Meeting the Challenge* (QCA, 2005b) recognizes that, while there is general consensus about the values, purposes and aims of the National Curriculum, there is also room for debate about the best way to organize learning to achieve our goals. It invited debate about the five challenges it set; how to respond to changes in society and the nature of work, the impact of technology, new understanding about learning, the need for greater personalization and innovation, and the increasing international dimensions of life and work. So we are invited to debate our responses to these challenges!

In 2006 Adamson, for The United Nations Children's Fund (Adamson, 2007), reported that children in the UK are more likely to suffer depression and anxiety than in any other western nation. We believe that this is not unrelated to a curriculum which does not heed the thinking of educational philosophers such as Dewey or take proper account of recent research. We explore the development of a curriculum through which children can develop their values relating to themselves, their community and the wider environment, through learning rigorously planned subjects appropriately linked.

In this book our examples illustrate how cross-curricular learning with history and geography at its heart can develop values associated with the key areas identified in the National Curriculum statement of values.

Each case study in the book uses a variety of types of enquiry and stimuli for enquiry. These offer different opportunities for children to learn in different ways. Each chapter, however, tends to focus on particular enquiries which have different characteristics. Some tend to lead to more logical thinking, others more aesthetic or ethical ideas and thoughts. (See Rowley, 2006, for a further discussion of types of enquiry.) Figure 1.2 shows how these enquiries lead to addressing different types of values.

It seems that the content is less important than the approach to enquiry in successful cross-curricular work. Furthermore the approach influences the way in which values are developed.

Cross-curricular learning, the humanities and values: an introduction to the case studies

Who am I? Valuing ourselves and others through thematic work in the Foundation Stage

This case study draws on all the Foundation Stage areas of learning. Jan Ashbridge and Jo Josephidou recognize the values already inherent in children's responses to unravelling the mysteries embedded in the 'unknown bear' and they connect these values to the curriculum that the Foundation Stage wishes to develop. In this chapter children explore values by drawing on all the areas of learning. In quoting Eaude they identify one of the key tensions that runs throughout this book, that of 'wishing to pass on one's own values, while recognising that children need to work out their own'. In many ways the recognition, in this chapter, of 'planned purposeful play' as the vehicle through which values are often developed in the Early Years Foundation Stage Framework (DfES, 2007) is not unrelated to the subsequent chapters where children's learning is often linked to what might be defined as 'play-like' activities, always based upon contexts which have been established by the teacher.

Jan and Jo here remind us that adopting a cross-curricular approach to learning will by definition be a social and a political decision and that, in consequence, values must be at the heart of such teaching and learning. While this has always been central to the Foundation Stage the connection has not always been made at Key Stages 2 and 3.

Where do I come from? History linked to mathematics, geography and language

In Chapter 3 Hugh Moore, in the context of a history-focused topic, gets right to the heart of values in history by asking the question 'where do we come from?' Central to the question is the nature of our origins and how that connects to our sense of nationhood and citizenship.

It is often assumed that the same values lie at the heart of history and the citizenship agenda and that values can be learned through history as a dimension of citizenship (see WM 1.3 for further discussion of citizenship and history).

Hugh Moore's chapter gives a useful case study of how good primary history can promote those values of an open society, and he does that through linking history with geography and mathematics in a way that is seamless, offering a model of cross-curricular learning where skills from other subjects support the understanding of our history.

Valuing my place: how can collaborative work with art help make the usual become unusual?

Central to much geography now is the increasing recognition that it is an understanding of our local place that is important in developing children's environmental values. Chris Barlow and Andrea Brooke in Chapter 4 work with a school over an intensive week looking at the development of values relating to place. Using art and geography they show how values are often best expressed though visual media and how good art can lead to good geography.

Slater (1996) argues that geography as a process and a discipline, is full of value-laden issues. Examples may be: respect for others, refusal to support values and actions which may harm individuals or communities, accepting responsibility to maintain a sustainable environment for future generations, responsibility for other species, issues concerned with development and with the balance and diversity of nature, preserving areas of beauty and repairing habitats damaged by human developments or natural disasters. In this chapter the children's own knowledge of their place becomes the vehicle through which their values are developed using a range of cross-curricular activities over an intensive week's work.

Valuing an unfamiliar place: promoting cross-curricular learning with ICT through a local school link

In Chapter 5 Rob Wheatley demonstrates how children's values in relation to a visit to an unfamiliar location often relate to and develop from 'powerful experiences' that we may not have foreseen; in this case the visit to a beach generated the context in which the children were able to talk about possible futures. The difficulty the children had in realistically thinking and talking about the future is not unusual, and perhaps raises the issue that children often have some difficulty with the future aspect of environmental education. How do we develop values for people who do not exist yet? In this example, involving a visit to Leigh-on-Sea, a short-term cross-curricular project comprising geography and ICT raises questions about the different ways that children perceive an unfamiliar location and the influence that this has on their tendency to see those who live there as living separate rather than parallel lives to their own. The dilemma is a familiar one to geographers teaching about place: on the one hand, wishing to develop a strong attachment to our place but, on the other, looking for ways of empathizing with other places. Rob Wheatley's use of ICT in this case study offers a useful way of expressing those thoughts.

Challenging our preconceived ideas: an alternative to Florence Nightingale for a history-focused cross-curricular theme with RE

In Chapter 6 Sue Temple works with teachers at Great Corby School, Cumbria, to introduce children to a Sufi Muslim mixed-race woman (Noor Inayat Khan) whose actions as a spy in the Second World War may challenge our preconceived ideas.

There is already plenty of evidence that young children are able to handle quite abstract and difficult materials by asking them how they would respond to dilemmas that come from the real world of history. Hilary Claire (2005), for example, offers an example where Year 5 children decide whether or not to help an escaped slave in the 1840s. (See WM 1.4 for more discussion of Hilary Claire's work.)

Chapter 6 supports Hilary Claire's findings that children can, given careful planning, understand the complexity of wider cultural and religious issues which challenge our preconceptions. In Sue Temple's chapter it becomes clear how subjects support each other. In Sue's words: 'The children needed both historical and religious skills, knowledge and understanding in order to benefit from the study of Noor Inayat Khan.'

Comparing my life with someone in the past: history, geography, ICT science and art

In Chapter 7 Jen Ager presents an excellent example of planning a theme on the Tudors in which the rigour of history is enhanced by its association with an intensive week of cross-curricular work. The results of that week can be seen on Teachers TV, along with an analytical video which identifies a number of key aspects of the planning which make it a good example of historical enquiry. (See WM 1.5 for further discussion of historical enquiry.)

Thinking through environmental values: geography, art and science

In Chapter 8 Chris Rowley reviews work by teachers and a National Trust Community Learning Officer on a project aimed at changing how the children think about their environment. The project contrasts with others by being run over a two-year period, enabling complex concepts to be returned to and developed in a range of different contexts and subjects. A feature of this chapter is that it identifies stages through which the children move in their understanding of concepts associated with the building of an eco-friendly school room in a piece of National Trust woodland. One danger is that a teacher may be strongly committed to one set of values and feel morally obliged to transmit them to the next generation, when the evidence is not complete, the issue is complex and there may be more than one perspective. So how can this be avoided, balancing commitment and neutrality? (See WM 1.6 for further discussion of the issue of balancing value positions in geography.)

What does it mean to be internationally minded at the age of 8? History and geography linked across the curriculum

In Chapter 9 Martin Skelton and Graham Reeves identify the possibilities and the dangers of using recent brain research in curriculum planning. In the International Primary Curriculum each subject is regarded as independent with its own learning goals. They are also, however, regarded as interdependent and children are taught to make connections, not just within the subjects but also between them in order to consolidate their learning. The chapter makes the important distinction between 'knowing' and 'understanding' and shows how the International Primary Curriculum sees the latter as a more likely outcome of well-planned cross-curricular learning. The example that they give of a class studying history without realizing it is history offers a perspective on cross-curricular learning which differs significantly from other approaches, including some of those seen in this book.

The global dimension involves such issues as conflict resolution, global citizenship, values and perceptions (WL 1.4). Fien (1996) considers that involvement with such issues also involves developing and applying personal qualities such as respect for others, and for human rights, compassion and concern for justice and open-mindedness. Chapter 9 raises interesting questions concerning the distinction between what Martin Skelton and Graham Reeves refer to as 'international mindedness' and 'global citizenship' discussed by Donna Hurford in Chapter 10.

Using dialogue to engage children with challenging ideas in cross-curricular work: geography and global citizenship across the curriculum through dialogue

In Chapter 10 Donna Hurford demonstrates how children in Year 6 engage with issues of social justice through cross-curricular sessions using a philosophy for children (P4C) approach. Dilemmas raised by the enquiries suggest that other dialogic approaches need to be used as well as P4C. It becomes clear, however, that there are aspects of the P4C approach, particularly in its power to bring together both rational and caring thinking, which give it a special role in the fusion of subjects surrounding all global citizenship questions. In many ways the chapter supports findings in Chapter 8 where children engaged with complex issues surrounding sustainability as a result of their use of P4C enquiry approaches.

A key element of this chapter is the range of stimuli that were used to develop the enquiries. These were adapted each week specifically in response to issues raised in the previous enquiry and included: a story; photographs and a wire toy; role play and, finally, a dilemma.

Planning for progression in values development in cross-curricular history and geography

It has been argued that values are embedded in both the enquiry process and the content of history and geography.

Figure 1.3 shows how progression in developing informed value judgements about the environment and the effects of changes in environments on the lives of people who live there is planned for,

	Questions	Investigations	Opinions
Level 1	Find answers to simple questions about the past	Use sources of information to answer simple questions	
Level 2	Observe or handle sources of information to answer questions about the past on the basis of simple observation	Recognise that their own lives are different from those in the past	Beginning to recognize there are reasons why people in the past acted as they did
Answer	To answer questions about the past	Use sources of information in ways that go beyond simple observation	Beginning to give a few reasons for, and results, of main events and changes
Level 4	Produce structured work	Begin to select and combine information from different sources	Give some reasons for, and the results, of main events and changes

Figure 1.3 Progression in developing informed value judgements in the National Curriculum Level Descriptors for History

monitored and assessed, in the National Curriculum Level Descriptors. Figure 1.3 traces development in understanding the reasons for changes, events and people's behaviour in past times through the History Level Descriptors.

We have considered the types of content teachers can plan for in order to encourage children to develop value-laden and informed opinions in history and geography. But what is the theoretical basis for planning for and monitoring progression in such thinking? What is 'moral development' and how is it linked to intellectual development? There is further discussion of this in WM 1.7.

The role of the teacher is to encourage the child to develop into the next stage of moral reasoning. This requires providing moral dilemmas for discussion, listening carefully to the children's reasoning, and creating a balance between letting children make decisions and challenging them in ways that show them the limitations of their thinking. Kohlberg et al. (1983) also said that children need experiences as well as reflection, to operate as moral agents in a community; this is reflected in the importance currently given to working with and in the family, school and community on, for example, environmental projects. Throughout this book teachers have identified key experiences to offer children the opportunities to reflect upon values in many different ways.

Assessment for values education and citizenship is also assessment for personal, moral, social and cultural development, and community involvement. Evidence for assessment in the context of value-laden issues discussed can be drawn from pupil reflection, teacher and learner observation and the quality of dialogue, both written and spoken. Of these, quality of dialogue is central. This includes listening as well as speaking. Personal reflection is also a key tool, for only the learner knows the quality of the feelings they may experience in relation to a value-laden issue, an unfairness or a perceived injustice.

At this interim stage it seems that the two Primary Reviews led by Alexander and Rose will endorse and recommend for primary educa-tion, the values underpinning the National Curriculum for England (DfEE/QCA, 1999), Assessment for Learning (Assessment Reform Group, 2002) and the *Big Picture* (QCA, 2008) will be upheld.

Assessment for Learning and values education

Assessment for Learning (AfL) is not value-free. It provides an approach to formative assessment that values the learner's holistic engagement with the learning and assessment process. 'Assessment for learning should recognise the full range of achievements of all learners' (Assessment Reform Group, 2002: 2).

The philosophy recommended through the *Big Picture* (QCA, 2008) supports the notion of looking at the whole child when evaluating the effectiveness of learning. Evaluating learning by looking for evidence of children's engagement with the whole learning process can encourage teachers and learners to be more aware of the breadth and scope of learning. Learning in a cross-curricular way can provide opportunities for breadth and scope that may not be possible through subject-based lessons. If teachers and learners are attuned to the possibility of 'unan-ticipated outcomes' (Steiner, 1993: 26), then the advantages of thematic approaches to teaching and learning become more apparent.

Abbs (cited in Barnes, 2007: 147) 'argues that without engagement there is no deep learning'. In line with this approach one of the 10 prin-ciples of AfL (Assessment Reform Group, 2002) identifies the need to involve learners with developing their own success criteria so they share an understanding of the learning process and can work towards their own goals. Clear and constructive feedback both from teachers and peers can help scaffold the learner's progress. The QCA (2008) recognizes the importance of involving children 'proactively with their learning'.

The assessment process advocated through AfL is presented as a confidence-building approach that can develop self-esteem and com-mitment to learning. If learners participate in identifying potential areas of learning this can help them recognize the relevance of certain skills, attitudes and knowledge. Offering children the opportunity to contextualize learning in meaningful experiences can encourage them to see themselves as lifelong learners.

Meta learning forms a significant part of AfL. Learners are encouraged to develop their 'capacity for self-assessment so that they can become reflective and self-managing' (Assessment Reform Group, 2002: 2). The notion of enabling children and young people to become independent learners with the confidence, skills and awareness to face future challenges is intrinsic to the *Big Picture* (QCA, 2008). If children are to engage with the learning process in a fulsome way then maybe Abbs's comment needs to be more fully embraced: 'Learning may be released by the teacher but it can never be conferred ... The student has to be the protagonist of his or her own learning' (2003, cited in Barnes, 2007: 147–8). Throughout the case studies examples will be found where teachers have used strategies to do just this.

References

Adamson, P. (2007) 'Child poverty in perspective: an overview of child well-being in rich countries', Innocenti Report Card 7, UNICEF Innocenti Research Centre, Florence. (Downloadable from: WL1.5 www.unicef-irc.org/publications/)

Assessment Reform Group (2002) *Assessment for Learning: 10 Principles. Research-Based Principles to Guide Classroom Practice.* London: London University Institute of Education.

Barnes, J. (2007) *Cross-curricular Learning 3–14.* London: Paul Chapman Publishing.

Bonnett, M. (2004) *Retrieving Nature: Education for a Post-humanist Age.* Oxford: Blackwell.

Claire, H. (2005) 'Learning and teaching about citizenship in the primary years', in *Leading Primary History.* London: Historical Association. pp. 24–43.

Declaration of Human Rights (1948) General Assembly of the United Nations Resolution, 217 A (111).

Department for Education and Employment/Qualifications and Curriculum Authority (DfEE/QCA) (1999) *The National Curriculum. Handbook for Teachers in England.* London: QCA.

Department for Education and Employment/Qualifications and Curriculum Authority (DfEE/QCA) (2003) *Excellence and Enjoyment: A Strategy for Primary Schools.* London: QCA.

Dewey, J. (1902) *The Child and the Curriculum.* Chicago, IL: University of Chicago Press.

Fien, J. (1996) 'Teaching to care: a case for commitment to teaching environmental values', in R. Gerber and J. Lidstone (eds), *Developments and Directions in Geographical Education.* Clevedon: Channel View Publications. pp. 77–92.

Hicks, D. (2007) 'Principles and Precedents', in D. Hicks and C. Holden, *Teaching the Global Dimension.* London: Routledge.

Kohlberg, L., Levine, C. and Hewer, A. (eds) (1983) *Moral Stages: A Current Formulation and a Response to Critics.* Basel and New York: Karger.

National Forum for Values in Education and the Community (1997) Accessible from the National Curriculum online website at WL 1.1.

Pike, G. and Selby, D. (2000) *In the Global Classroom.* 2 vols. Toronto: Pippin Press.

Qualifications and Curriculum Authority (QCA) (2005a) *Every Child Matters and Youth Matters.* London: QCA.

Qualifications and Curriculum Authority (QCA) (2005b) *The Futures Programme: Meeting the Challenge.* London: QCA.

Qualifications and Curriculum Authority (QCA) (2008) *Big Picture.* April–June. Available at WL 1.6. (Accessed 28 July 2008.)

Rowley, C. (2006) 'Are there different types of geographical enquiry?', in H. Cooper, C. Rowley and S. Asquith, *Geography 3–11.* London: Routledge. pp. 17–32.

Slater, F. (1996) 'Values: towards mapping their locations in a geography education', in A. Kent, D. Lambert, M. Naish and F. Slater (eds), *Geography in Education: Viewpoints on Teaching and Learning.* Cambridge: Cambridge University Press. pp. 200–30.

Steiner, M. (1993) *Learning from Experience. World Studies in the Primary Classroom.* Stoke-on-Trent: Trentham Books.

2

Who am I? How can we learn to value ourselves and others through thematic work supporting the development of children's knowledge and understanding of the world in the Foundation Stage?

Jan Ashbridge and Jo Josephidou

Chapter introduction

Jan Ashbridge of the University of Cumbria works with Jo Josephidou of St Bernadette's School, Lancaster, to investigate how the Foundation Stage curriculum often provides us with excellent examples of the development of values through the humanities. Specifically they look at how children with English as a second language demonstrate a wealth of knowledge about other countries, and how their values develop as this knowledge is assimilated.

Introduction: a mission statement

In the rush towards planning for learning through cross-curricular themes that is currently happening in primary schools, some staff are scratching their heads and wondering what all the fuss is about. These are, more often than not, the practitioners who work with the youngest children in the Nursery or Reception classes, for whom the subject-specific nature of the National Curriculum and the strategies have either been of minimal impact, or have been adapted and developed to suit particular philosophies and pedagogies. For us (nailing our colours firmly to the mast), children, rather than the curriculum subjects, are at the heart of what happens. The needs of the children, rather than attainment targets, determine any intended learning, and the interests of the children steer the learning experiences on offer.

When supporting the learning and development of very young children, practitioners need to be able to understand the way in which these children interact with and understand the world around them. Children learn through everything they see, hear, smell, touch and taste in the environment and experiences provided. Their learning 'is not compartmentalised' and they learn through making 'connections between experiences and ideas ... related to any aspect of their life' (DfES/QCA, 2000: 45). Thus an obvious solution is an integrated approach to children's learning and practitioners' planning, in a way that is currently familiar in the Early Years.

A recognition of how young children learn is very important; but perhaps of more importance to the children themselves is a knowledge that they are valued and understood as individuals.

Knowing me, knowing you

In the previous chapter, Chris Rowley and Hilary Cooper group values into three categories: those relating to self and individual learning; those that relate to relationships, community and collaborative learning; and those relating to the environment. Looking at these, it would appear that an appropriate Early Years curriculum is naturally a values-based curriculum as it seeks to support children in developing 'a positive sense of themselves and others' (DfES, 2007a: 22).

When asked what we teach, we reply 'children' – the whole child and all the wonderful complexity that that encompasses. By truly starting from the child in our practice, we are embracing them holistically. This must start with helping the children to find out who they are and to value themselves. The Geographical Association recognizes this when they state that 'young children learn best when they feel valued [and] secure ... [when] the child is valued for who she or he is' (Martin and Owens, 2004: 64).

Feeling valued and confident will lead to children having positive self-regard and self-esteem. This sense of self-worth supports the development of positive attitudes to themselves as learners; enabling children to interact positively with their environment and the other people who inhabit it. The values that children develop will reflect and structure the kind of people they will become. It seems vital therefore to acknowledge the tensions identified by Eaude (2008: 20) but recognized by all who work in this field: 'wishing to pass on one's own values, while recognising that children need to work out their own'. It is ultimately the children, not the adults who work with them, who will choose the types of people they become. Our settings, even our Early Years settings, are, therefore, social and even political spaces. Invernizzi and Williams (2008: 23) argue persuasively that politics is our values and attitudes in practice. Teaching young children (in the holistic sense), therefore, means that any curriculum offered to them needs to have values at the heart of it as these will inform how the setting operates and how the children will treat and see each other within that environment. Through practitioners acknowledging and respecting children's own values and showing them respect, children are helped to value and accept others in positive ways.

This will not happen automatically. Practitioners must 'model the value that they place on the lives and backgrounds of others' (Martin and Owens, 2004: 64). The role, according to Eaude (2008: 58), is to help, support and guide children in creating their own identity and character by providing a 'framework of values'.

Vygotsky believed that children were 'cultural apprentices' (May et al., 2006: 11). This has obvious implications for practitioners in terms of the discussion around values and the inculcation of young children into the world of education and the wider society. The curriculum offered will very much depend on the values and beliefs of the practitioner; it will reflect their attitudes and philosophy.

The play's the thing

May et al. (2006: 38) describe an Early Years curriculum as being 'a course of action that is carried out for reasons that best serve the desired outcome of providing children with what they need'. This begs the question 'How do we know what they need?'

For learning to be meaningful it needs to be set in a context which recognizes children's social and emotional needs, their interests, and their need to actively engage and participate in their learning and learning environment. Children learn, as pointed out earlier, in a holistic way. Subject boundaries mean very little to our youngest children, so meaningful learning for them is less about us passing on pieces of pre-planned information in a structured format, and more about being able to deal with what, for them, must surely be a constantly changing, evolving environment in which they must make decisions, solve problems and interact. We want them to think about thinking and learning and how their learning is developing and moving on, as they build new ideas from their existing understanding, 'through continuous, developmental, experiential learning ... [which] places the child ... at the heart of the process' (May et al., 2006: 101–2).

The Early Years Foundation Stage (EYFS) framework (DfES, 2007b) helps practitioners to organize their thinking about children's learning and development by linking concepts and skills to Areas of Learning and Development, one of which, 'Knowledge and understanding of the world', brings together certain ideas which children use to try and make sense of the world around them. As discrete subject disciplines, both history and geography make claims that the skills and concepts embedded within their subject are able to best help children to identify with others, acquire understanding and respect and understand themselves (Geographical Association, in Martin and Owens, 2004: 64; Hazareesingh et al., 1994: 3; National Curriculum Council, 1991). It is necessary, however, to keep at the front of our minds the fact that these 'boundaries' are primarily for our benefit and that children's learning is not linear and does not easily fit into categories. Any curriculum can be seen as having two interfaces. There is the, hopefully, seamless, boundary-free experience of the child who is enabled to explore their own interests in a way that best suits them, and the more structured, planned experience of the practitioner who is aware of the rationale behind the organization, resources and the learning experiences on offer to the children. The careful observation, reflection, discussion, thought and planning that goes on behind the scenes is instrumental in ensuring that children's needs are met and that any learning they choose to be engaged in is offered within a context that is meaningful to the child, helping them to best make connections between previous experiences and new learning.

It is through a play-based curriculum that these meaningful contexts can be developed and supported. The EYFS framework statutorily requires practitioners to deliver their curriculum through 'planned purposeful play' and through a balance of 'adult-led and child-initiated' experiences and activities (DfES, 2007b: 11).

It is through play that children are able to bring together and consolidate concepts and skills, and form them into experiences where they are in control and can therefore spend the time getting to grips with 'sorting out their lives and making new sense of what surrounds them' (Gooch, 2006: 180).

Supporting children's learning in a holistic way through a play-based curriculum helps practitioners to concentrate on creating contexts for learning in which children are 'able to participate increasingly effectively in the world in which [they] find [them]selves' (Anning and Edwards, 2006: 57).

Who's in charge?

'Children are much more involved in the task, and more competent in devising and using strategies, when they work on problems that they themselves have set' (Bruner and Haste, 1993: 13, in de Boo, 2004: 12). This presents a challenge for practitioners as it appears we must be clear about what true play is and what is an adult-directed activity, no matter how playful it appears. It is easier for practitioners to shape and structure children's play experiences, as this gives reassurance that their own targets have been met and children helped to meet theirs. Measurability is, therefore, built in. However, as David (2001: 55) so succinctly puts it, 'didactic, teacher planned instruction has no part in an early years teacher's repertoire – is in fact a waste of time – because children learn best through "hands on" self chosen play experiences'. This strongly worded view does not perhaps reflect the pedagogy of the majority of Early Years practitioners but it illustrates a point that all educators will hopefully agree with, that children develop knowledge in contexts *they* understand and are meaningful to *them*. The importance of child-initiated and -led play cannot be underestimated. It is in this play and in the discussions, and conversations with peers and adults that are part of it, that the real learning and understanding of the children is glimpsed. Children will try to link their limited perceptions and experiences with the environment they are familiar with, and through this make and test hypotheses on which to base their new and developing knowledge, concepts and understandings (Ashbridge, 2006: 116). This is discussed again later in this chapter. Wood and Attfield remind practitioners that 'children do not just play with objects and materials: they also play with meanings, ideas, roles, rules and relationships and can make significant cognitive leaps and transformations' (2005: 43).

A balance is obviously needed. Practitioners cannot simply be passive, as children will not be able to reach their full potential. Neither should they engage in traditional styles of direct instruction which Meade (1999), in May et al. (2006: 42), identifies as being counterproductive. Supporting children's developing understanding requires practitioners to be 'sensitively proactive' (May et al., 2006: 42). The observation and planning cycle (Figure 2.1) offered by the EYFS (DfES, 2007b) helps practitioners to tune in to what is important to children, how they are choosing to take their own learning forwards and then, after reflection, plan experiences, modifications to the learning environment and sensitive interventions. Knowledge of children, not knowledge of the curriculum, then feeds the next steps in learning.

It is within this context, and with this philosophy, that the following project was developed. It has been a collaboration between a class-based Reception teacher and her team, and a senior lecturer in Early Childhood Education from one of the local universities.

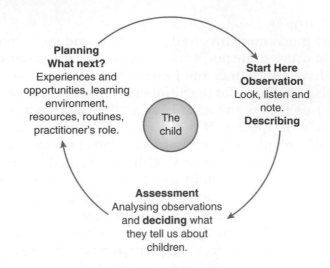

Figure 2.1   The Early Years and Foundation Stage planning cycle

All about us

The project was carried out at a small Roman Catholic primary school in the north-west of England. It is set in a middle-class suburb of a small city. Because of its close proximity to two universities, it also has a high proportion of children who have English as an additional language (EAL), and its reputation as a caring, inclusive school has led to a higher than average proportion of children who have specific, individual needs. The cultures and languages brought to the school are celebrated in the Reception class and often become the focus of teaching and learning. Some children are already, at the age of 5, trilingual and are participating in their third cultural experience of education, so they bring a stronger and more developed knowledge base about the world to the classroom than do their peers and have a very different understanding of the world than do the local children, many of whom have not even visited their own capital city. The fact that it is a Roman Catholic primary school with a staff highly committed to the Christian ethos of the school could be a source of potential conflict as many other faiths and cultures are represented there by children and parents. However both staff and parents work successfully together to embed a shared sense of values where 'every child matters'.

Who do we think we are?
This project was inspired by a popular television programme which takes celebrity adults on a journey to explore their roots and consider what makes them who they are today. Young children are on a constant

quest to find out who they are. This is at the core of the Early Years Foundation Stage framework. They learn the following:

- to have a developing awareness of their own needs, views and feelings, and be sensitive to the needs, views and feelings of others
- to have a developing respect for their own cultures and beliefs, and those of other people
- to understand that people have different needs, views, cultures and beliefs, which need to be treated with respect
- that they can expect others to treat their needs, views, cultures and beliefs with respect
- to look for similarities and differences
- to know about their own cultures and beliefs and those of other people (a selection of Early Learning Goals from DfES, 2007a).

The key questions inspired by the television programme are noteworthy.

- Where was I born?
- Where do my parents come from?
- What kind of community do I live in?
- What is my faith?
- What does it say on my passport?

Would it be possible then to take the key questions inspired by the programme and use them in an exciting, creative and thematic way to enable children to consider similarities and differences between themselves and others? Could they thus learn to value themselves and others while developing their knowledge and understanding of the world?

The project began with a teddy bear, wearing a parachute; it was found hanging from a tree in the school garden. He was rescued by the children and taken back to the classroom where they hypothesized about who he was, how he had got stuck in a tree and who he belonged to. The children searched thoroughly to see if they could find his name anywhere but all to no avail. They were already familiar with toys communicating by whispering in the teacher's ear, a teaching and learning device often employed in the Early Years setting.

This bear, however, could neither understand what the teacher and children were saying nor communicate in a language that the teacher could understand. Because of the diverse cultural mix of the class and the high priority given to valuing and using the languages that the children speak, it was quickly established that the bear was not French, Spanish, Polish, German, Italian, Korean, Greek or Nigerian. He was, however, carrying a small bag and the children were encouraged to be 'detectives' and look for any clues in his bag which would shine some kind of light on his identity. None of the clues carried any written reference that the children could decode, but they did have a Chinese theme (coins, passport, photographs, chopsticks, food, world map, prayer wheel, calligraphy brush), so initial cross-curricular planning had this theme at its core. However as every Early Years practitioner will know, once the stimulus for learning has been provided, it is vital that assessment for learning takes place and the children are carefully observed to see where their learning is taking them, and thus provision for the next vital step can be made. Effective teaching and learning happens in Early Years settings when the practitioner participates in quality 'sustained shared thinking' (Siraj-Blatchford et al., 2002: 11) with either groups or individual children and refuses to stick rigidly to initial planning, but constantly modifies it in line with children's interests and attainment.

This particular stimulus was chosen because it was felt it would grab the children's attention and motivate them into wanting to find out more about the bear. It was hoped that it would tap into their 'innate interest in novelty' which 'motivates them to explore' and 'for Piaget, this exploration is a cognitive process closely linked to the development of intelligence' (Voss and Keller, 1983; cited in Chak, 2007: 142–3).

Careful, detailed observation of the class throughout the year had left the classroom practitioner with a thorough knowledge of what would engage and excite the children both as a group and as individuals (DfES, 2007(b): 16). It would lead to purposeful activities where children could use emerging literacy and numeracy skills in a meaningful way and provide lots of opportunities for talking, discussion and collaborative learning. In the race to get the children reading and writing, speaking and listening activities can often be thrown in as an afterthought, but the reflective practitioner celebrates the power of the spoken language and provides as many opportunities as possible for the children to develop their reasoning skills through talking to and listening to their peers. Indeed, the EYFS framework consistently reminds us of the importance of children discussing, speculating, describing, predicting and supporting each other's learning and understanding (DfES, 2007a: 76). It is through observing these interactions and activities that the practitioner can build up a detailed picture of each child's knowledge and understanding of the world and the links they are making in their learning, thereby providing for the next step.

The values that this particular Foundation Stage practitioner wishes to impart through the teaching and learning are these:

Communication, language and literacy	Creative development	Personal social and emotional development

• Opportunities for critical thinking and problem-solving in role play. How can the children provide a home which will meet the needs of the bear and how will they look after him and communicate with him?
 	
 • Making passports and writing posters to help find the owner of the bear
 	
 • Writing captions for photos of China
 	
 • Looking at non-fiction books on China and traditional Chinese stories
	• Using black paint and calligraphy brushes to write some Chinese letters
	
	 • Exploring red, black and gold materials
	
	 • Mixing powder paints to replicate Chinese watercolours and making own scrolls
		• Use talk partners to explore how the bear must be feeling. What makes them happy and sad? How can they look after the bear and help him to feel happy? What are his needs?
		
		 • What kind of community do they live in? What are their beliefs?
		   • How do we show respect to others?
		   • Explore idea that different is not wrong

The Unknown Bear

Problem-solving, reasoning and numeracy	Knowledge and understanding of the world	Physical development
• Looking at different number systems and learning to count in Chinese and other languages • Writing numbers in Chinese • Sequencing activities to develop vocabulary of time • Measuring to make things for Bear's home • Measuring and counting and problem-solving through the setting up of a mini Olympics	• Comparing their lunch box with boxes containing food from different cultures, with opportunities to smell and taste the food • Observing how noodles change when they are put in hot water • Opportunities to use cooking equipment in role play that reflects different cultures, e.g. wok, chopsticks • Making map to help Bear get home and problem-solving: which countries does he pass over? How will he travel? • Visit to local Chinese supermarket and buy food that Bear will like • Setting up Chinese restaurant in role play • Looking for similarities and differences as we explore who is this Bear? And who are we? • Using Internet to find out about China and route the Bear has travelled • Examine photos of Chinese architecture and use construction to explore these shapes and structures • Make 3D representations of Bear's journey	• Dressing-up clothes to reflect different cultures • Using dough to make noodles • Learning to use chopsticks • Explore different ways of moving to Chinese music

Key vocabulary: needs, feelings, communicate, care for, community beliefs, believe, faith, respect, similarities, differences, different, same, compare

Figure 2.2 The initial planning that took place

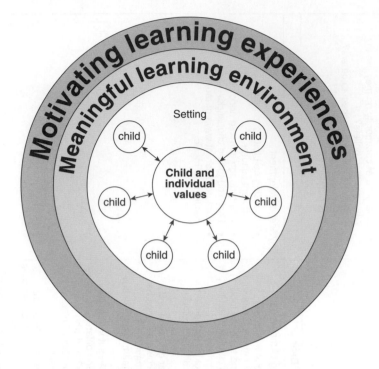

Figure 2.3   A model to illustrate the influences on children's values in the classroom

- Everybody has a contribution to make; we are all teachers and learners.
- Everybody has the ability to succeed, and steps taken in personal and social skills are praised as highly as those made in reading and writing.
- Everyone needs to take responsibility for their own learning and behaviour, and adults *and peers* in the setting are there to support you and guide you in taking this responsibility.
- We all have a responsibility towards others in our class, to look after them and help them succeed, both academically and socially.

Figure 2.3 is an attempt to show the various influences on children's ability to recognize and value themselves and the attitudes and beliefs that they bring to the setting. Through developing this understanding, children gain in confidence and self-esteem, which helps them to begin to reach out to others in their immediate environment with empathy and a degree of understanding. The practitioner can support this 'theory of mind' (Anning and Edwards, 2006: 72); helping children to recognize, through a supportive and inclusive learning environment, that others will see things differently from themselves and will have different understandings and beliefs. Such a learning environment is one in which all children can recognize something of themselves and their background. Within that environment, children need to have access to motivating learning experiences which are challenging but where children can succeed at their own level. In this way, the practitioner is playing her part in shaping the children's values and beliefs, while encouraging the children to take responsibility for their own attitudes.

The project represented here – 'the unknown bear' – was planned to last for up to half a term. It was building on experiences in the previous half-term which used Persona dolls to explore similarities, differences and the conflict that might arise because of this. Information was collected by either observing the children working independently or in a focused group with an adult. On other occasions the classroom practitioner would work with small or large groups and write up her observations in diary form after the event. Time constraints meant that although the unit was planned to last for about six weeks the observations used for this chapter focus on two weeks only.

Listening to the children

The greatest revelation for the practitioner was the amount of knowledge that children with English as an Additional Language (EAL) in particular had at their disposal. These were often children who had needed much more support than others in developing literacy and social skills but suddenly they were the experts. The impact of having a platform from which to share their knowledge meant they were constantly having to use language to explain and hypothesize, developing their ability to articulate in English and thus make connections in their learning which took their thinking on to a higher level.

It took S about 2 minutes to look at Bear's passport and declare: 'I know he's from China … L writes like that …'. S, a Spanish speaker, has already lived in Holland and the USA. She lives on the university campus and refers to L, a neighbour who had invited her round for a meal. S could describe how to use chopsticks and was familiar with Chinese cooking. Often quite shy in class, S can be easily intimidated by other children; however her understanding of the world and eagerness to articulate this knowledge is highly developed. She also demonstrated a considerable ability to empathize with other cultures and celebrate their differences. This was apparent when the children were comparing their own packed lunch with Bear's.

A: I don't eat food I haven't had before.
S: It's spicy … I like spicy food … I love it … my next door neighbour
          has this.
D: I only eat English meatballs. (This from a child who is actually
          Polish.)
Teacher: I could tell by your face you didn't like it … why?
B: It's not like my pack lunch … I like something like I have … ham …
          jelly … yoghurt and stuff.
Teacher: Do you think Bear would like your packed lunch?
B: No I eat English food … he's from another country.
S: Yes he would like your food … my country's food is chocolate …
          but I like pizza … there's no pizza where it's cold where the
          penguins live.

J, also trilingual, recognized some of the photographs of China: 'It's the great big wall from China … it's very, very big.' *J* also pondered on why the Bear had come to this particular place: 'I know why the bear came … it exploded … the buildings came crashing down', presumably a reference to the recent earthquake in China which he must have seen on the television at home. This was particularly interesting as *J* originally comes from an East Asian country and may perhaps have been more sensitive to this particular event than most children, due to perceived similarities in the culture.

R, who is monolingual but who had recently moved to the north of England from near London, also had a more highly developed knowledge of the world than many of his classmates even though he had been in full-time education for a much shorter time: 'Chinese people eat noodles and they use chopsticks … you have to cook them first … instead of writing in English they write in pictures … '. He was particularly motivated by this project as, even though he was new to the class, he had something to contribute immediately. He was able, as indeed all the children were, to look for similarities and differences between himself and the bear, and consequently between himself and his new classmates.

It was hardly surprising, though remarkable to see in action, how the children problem-solved, not only by making links with what they had already learnt about the world but also by referring to issues which were uppermost in their minds at the time, as if in problem-solving about the bear they were also able to explore other issues that were concerning them.

F, for example, who was missing family members who had gone to live in Australia, referred everything back to this: 'In Australia they do writing like that and it's got a picture of Australia … '. Another child, *M*, referred everything back to her grandmother: 'My nana uses chopsticks … my nana likes that food … '. Or *N*, when looking at the photographs, declared: 'it's where he lives or where he's been on holiday … maybe he didn't like the food'.

We can again mention *J* here. His concern over the earthquake was obviously at the front of his mind as he tried to think why someone from China might suddenly be found in England. This was his first thought.

And, of course, when the children were questioned on the sex of the bear, all of the boys felt it was a boy:

J: He looks like a boy … girls have long hair.
D: A boy because of his nose …
M: A boy … his black nose … a blue bag … he might be a boy …

Whereas the girls felt it was female:

N: … a girl … a bit of pink on his (*sic*) bag … he likes green … I do too.
S: … a girl … look at the yellow and red
Z: … a girl … her bag.

Another interesting observation was that if the children did not recognize an artefact they were almost unanimous in declaring that it was 'something from the olden days'. When questioned further on this they gave various reasons:

M: I think these things are olden day things … they have loads of scratches and fingerprints.
K: It's very old because it's scraped.
M: It stayed very long in the rain … they are all very old … they are not ours … it smells like when it was first used … they smell like when they are old.
N: Inside it's dusty.

Their understanding of the olden days varied:

M: It was then you need fire to put light … candles
K: The olden days is not like now … children were allowed to act at the circus. (I think this was said rather wistfully!)

What does this mean about young children's understanding of specific historical and geographical concepts? There is obviously an issue here. A clue to this lies in the fact that the EYFS does not, in fact, set out to overtly help teachers to teach history or geography. It supports children's developing 'Knowledge and understanding of the world'. This more holistic title does more than simply provide a convenient title under which to place these concepts and understandings. It reflects the way in which children experience and make sense of the unfamiliar. They try to latch new knowledge and information onto something that they already know. In this case, unfamiliar things that the practitioner gives them to look at are probably from past times. The actual skills that are required to find out about the objects are the same, regardless of whether they look at them from a historical (time) or a geographical (place) or even from a scientific (exploration and investigation) point of view. (The parenthetic words refer to some of the different aspects identified under 'Knowledge and understanding of the world'.) These skills are demonstrated here as the children try to solve the problem of what these things are and where or when they come from. They are investigating using all their senses, observing, comparing, discussing differences and making connections. The fact that they opt for a historical context rather than a geographical one is because 'time and place are both concepts that it is hard to experience directly and require a lot of imagination and empathy to develop' (Ashbridge, 2006: 123). At this age children develop these skills of empathy and imagination through play and discussion, and, with maturity and greater experience, children are able to hone these generic skills and apply them in the right context more often. What is encouraging in this situation is that the children knew which skills to use.

Was the learning transformative?

Children clearly added more pieces to the jigsaw of the idea they are building up about the world. These were positive, colourful pieces to counteract the constant bombardment of ideas about how the world is such a negative, frightening place that we constantly attempt to shelter our children from. They were able to develop their ability to articulate their views and also listen to the views of others, at the same time as realizing that we all have something to learn from those around us. The balance of power in the relationships of the class shifted slightly as quieter children shared their knowledge with more confident children. This demonstrates the empowering nature of learning when children are supported in developing their ability to link one part of their life experience to another as part of this planned project. All Areas of Learning and Development were encompassed and developed in an unforced and (as far as the children were concerned) unstructured way. It was their responses to experiences, activities and discussions that shaped the way the project developed; their questions and the problems they set themselves which directed the learning outcomes. This approach is reminiscent of Dewey's idea which was 'to value children's experience as the starting point for developing or constructing new ideas, rather than assuming there is an absence of knowledge for the teacher to fill' (May et al., 2006: 102).

Reflections from the classroom

As a practitioner, I have been reminded of how important it is to constantly 'look for the novelty' to inspire and motivate children and help them reveal better their knowledge and understanding of the world. Our planning can often be determined by what has worked well before, but higher-level thinking and learning happens with our youngest children (and perhaps all our children) when the planning is dynamic, based on intelligent observations and effective pupil–teacher dialogue. It is worth remembering that the practitioner is also on a learning journey. I have been reminded also, that just as with number and literacy skills, there can be a very wide gap between the most and least 'able' children in the class, there also exists this wide gap in 'Knowledge and understanding of the world' which is not necessarily determined by academic ability or the ability to read and write. The challenge is to narrow the gap and to support children with good skills in making sense of the world around them, and to use these to access the whole curriculum more successfully.

More reflections

The class of children involved in this project were from a diverse range of backgrounds and cultures, with the diverse range of values and attitudes that this implies. A bear was chosen as the stimulus as it has a universal familiarity which bridges the different life experiences of the children. It is through building on the known that children are able to add to their understanding and take their learning forward. What better than a bear to help children go from the familiar to the unfamiliar? Piaget's ideas of assimilation and accommodation are helpful here. Much of children's play is assimilation where they become familiar with aspects, objects and concepts about their world. This is a key way that children make sense of their world. Sometimes new information is acquired that means children have to alter the way they view and understand the world (accommodation). Assimilation and accommodation often occur together when a child is using their existing understandings and adjusts this to cope with new information. There is a balance between what is understood and what is experienced. The bear could have come from anywhere, Pluto, Luton or Oslo. The place was not important – just the fact that it was not here. China was selected because it was a place and culture of which none of the children had any first-hand knowledge. All the children would be at a similar level of experience. Even though they were ostensibly exploring the background of the 'unknown bear', they were actually engaged in thinking about where *they* were from and what was important to each of *them*. They did this through trying to make sense of and empathize with the experience of the bear. Doing this meant that they had to explore and examine difference, between them and the bear and between each other. The playful, play-based and child-initiated learning that came from this, supported them in exploring and understanding more about the world of the bear and, by association, their own world and that of others around them.

Knowledge and understanding of the world and core values

The emerging values which the children were exploring were their own identities, valuing themselves and each other, valuing their own culture and that of a community they live in. These values are thoroughly interpreted with concepts of embryonic time and place, of similarities and differences between then and now, here and there.

References

Anning, A. and Edwards, A. (2006) *Promoting Children's Learning from Birth to Five*. 2nd edn. Maidenhead: Open University Press.

Ashbridge, J. (2006) 'Is geography suitable for the Foundation Stage?', in H. Cooper, S. Asquith and C. Rowley (eds), *Geography 3–11: A Guide for Teachers*. London: Taylor Francis. pp. 115–27.

Chak, A. (2007) 'Teachers' and parents' conceptions of children's curiosity and exploration', *International Journal of Early Years Education*, 15(2): 141–59.

David, T. (2001) 'Curriculum in the Early Years', in G. Pugh (ed.), *Contemporary Issues in the Early Years*. 3rd edn. London: Paul Chapman Publishing. pp. 55–65.

De Boo, M. (2004) *The Early Years Handbook*. Sheffield: Geographical Association.

Chak, A., (2007) Teachers' and parents' conceptions of children's curiosity and exploration in International Journal of Early Years Education 15:2, 141–15

Department for Education and Employment/Qualifications and Curriculum Authority (DfEE/QCA) (2000) *Curriculum Guidance for the Foundation Stage*. London: DfEE/QCA.

Department for Education and Skills (DfES) (2007a) *Practice Guidance for the Early Years Foundation Stage*. Nottingham: DfES.

Department for Education and Skills (DfES) (2007b) *Statutory Framework for the Early Years Foundation Stage*. Nottingham: DfES.

Eaude, T. (2008) *Children's Spiritual, Moral, Social and Cultural Development*. 2nd edn. Exeter: Learning Matters.

Gooch, K. (2006) 'Supporting children's development and learning', in T. Bruce (ed.), *Early Childhood*. London: Sage. pp. 173–89.

Hazareesingh, S., Kenway, P. and Simms, K. (1994) *Speaking about the Past*. Stoke-on-Trent: Trentham Books.

Invernizzi, A. and Williams, J. (ed.) (2008) *Children and Citizenship*. London: Sage.

Martin, F. and Owens, P. (2004) 'Young children making sense of their place in the world', in S. Scoffham (ed.), *Primary Geography Handbook*. Sheffield: Geographical Association. pp. 63–91.

May, P., Ashford, E. and Bottle, G. (2006) *Sound Beginnings*. London: David Fulton.

National Curriculum Council (1991) *History: Non-Statutory Guidance*. York: National Curriculum Council.

Siraj-Blatchford, I., Sylva, K., Muttock, S., Gilden, R. and Bell, D. (2002) *Researching Effective Pedagogy in the Early Years*. Research Report No. 356. London: DfES.

Wood, E. and Attfield, J. (2005) *Play, Learning and the Early Childhood Curriculum*. 2nd edn. London: Paul Chapman Publishing.

3

Where do I come from? History linked to mathematics, geography and language

Hugh Moore

This chapter is in memory of my wife and mother of our three sons, Ginny

---

Chapter introduction

In this chapter Hugh Moore works with Sue Wilcock of Tatham Fells school near Lancaster and Emily Lyons of St Mary's, Kirkby Lonsdale, to enable children to identify the values that underpin our own view of who we are. They propose using cross-curricular learning to enable children to address these deeply held values through a range of activities which engage the children in a genuine historical enquiry. Mathematics plays a particularly important role in developing further the concept of time lines.

On the Monday of this themed week each group of children involved is given an envelope (detailing the work they must do) but they are not allowed to open it until Thursday. The early part of the week is spent preparing for the task – which is titled, 'Who are We Really'? – by doing some suggested activities on the 'Invaders and Settlers' theme.

Creating a themed week of teaching on history is an enticing prospect – for some of us at least – but creating and maintaining that theme in a meaningful way is not easy; less easy when an essential part of the week is to reflect on the shared cultural values and ideas we have about who we really are.

(Continued)

(Continued)

This idea is conceptual and could be used within a thematic history project; as a group develops their understanding of the Ancient Egyptians, the Sumerians or the Greeks, for example. It would be a vital part of such a thematic study to make a comparison with life in ancient and modern Britain, and to reflect on how progress within those distant societies has touched our lives. This should be done because – to paraphrase Douglas Adams – it is about 'the fundamental interconnectedness of all things'. In other words the British might have invented spinning machines, radar, the telephone, the computer, and so on, but if other cultures had not already come up with farming, writing, mathematics, time, making metal, civilization and similar developments, then the spinning machine would not have been much good anyway.

Concepts, 'cross-curricularity' and the history of the north

The main concept to be explored is the impact of those peoples on the society, culture, religions and language that we share now. This is inclusion with a difference – this includes us all because it is about origins. Fullinwider (2006), in a paper discussing the rise of multicultural education in the USA, talks about the valuing of cultural groups. He relates aspects of the Maryland code: that students should value their own heritage, respect the uniqueness of cultures other than their own and understand the richness of cultural diversity and the meaning of commonality. This has been partly my maxim in the writing of this piece; the richness and diversity of this society has grown because of the waves of settlers and invaders and our absorption of ideas from other places. He goes on to tell us that multicultural literature urges us to explore the contributions that different groups have made to contemporary society, and the importance of seeing events from multiple perspectives. As Grosvenor (1997) reminds us, people from the minorities are all too often seen as deviants from the norm but in fact (my words) they are part of the norm. But this is not about understanding and valuing other cultures; it is about thinking about 'our own'. It is about asking the question 'Who are we? NO – WHO ARE WE REALLY?' Where does our culture come from? Where do our genes come from? Are we not all from different minorities? Grosvenor goes on to point out that modern alien cultures are seen to have threatened our own. This project encourages us to think about this perceived threat by asking, 'Who brought our culture and was it ours anyway?'. Grosvenor talks about narratives of British history and the relationship between history and identity. I think about it like this. I am white, English and, to make matters 'worse', middle class, but the maiden names of my respective grandmothers (Tudgy and Bellew) imply a possible Norman connection, while my own surname, Moore, may imply that one of my ancestors may have been an African slave or (less likely in my case) Irish. Fantastic, but does it matter? Yes it does because my story simply is not much different from the rest of the population.

So how about a quick history lesson to illustrate what I mean? As I write this I'm sitting in the North, Cumbria actually, and I know that archaeological evidence supports the notion that nobody lived up here before 11,000 years ago – around the time the world's earliest town was appearing (Jericho). The reason for this absence of people is simple – ice. The last Ice Age was in the process of melting and the British Isles simply were not habitable. Not that there were not people here long before that, but it was a mobile population, one that ebbed and flowed. Pryor (2004) quotes Don Bothwell's estimate that the British population during the so called Lower Palaeolithic would have been fewer than 5,000 and Chris Smith's estimate (although Pryor thinks this is low) is that it would probably have been little more in 5000 BC by which time the huge town at Çatal Hüyük in Anatolia was already some 2,000 years old.

Where do our ideas about history come from?

McGuinn (2002) reminds us that part of the powerful metanarrative which lies in western thought is contained in the Bible. He goes on to remind us that classical ideas too form part of our cultural roots. I will return to his thinking later, but this reminder is timely – our cultural heritage is not quite the same as our people heritage, and that can make the past difficult to understand. What I mean by this is that while we can link some of our thinking on law to Cicero and our thinking on science to Archimedes, and so on, our people heritage comes from other directions.

Those of you who remember Julian Richard's BBC series, *The Blood of the Vikings* (2001), will recall his search for our people's heritage through David Goldstein's search for Viking DNA in our blood. People heritage is different, it is about our genes, it is about the genesis of the language we speak and it is about wondering about the people who gave these things to us. What were they like? How can we trace them?

How and why should we do anything about them in the small space of a primary classroom?

History in the primary classroom

we wanted to equip those pupils who have special learning needs with several qualities: the necessary life skill of critical thinking, a rich understanding of the world in which they live and the values needed to enjoy and respect our diverse society. (Philpott, 2008: 84)

Joanne Philpott is telling us that she wants her pupils – who, incidentally, are about to be excluded from doing history at KS3 because of their special needs – to have a feel for history, to get a 'sense of time, place and purpose'. She goes on to say that because history is taught thematically it is difficult for her pupils to develop chronological understanding. She wants to help give her pupils – the ones who are about to be deprived – 'a sense of the purpose of history in their future lives'.

This, however, is true for all pupils, especially at KS2, for if history has no purpose, it is valueless; if history does not help the pupils to see themselves and their ancestors in the context of time, it is irrelevant.

Disembedded thinking, Margaret Donaldson tells us, is at its most powerful when combined with doing (Donaldson, 1985). She is reminding us that the mind is connected to the body and that we are better at reasoning than we are at talking human sense. History, as I have just shown, is cognitively complicated; it is about attaching hugely different strands of evidence together to make a big story. The reasoning involved is often deep, complicated and removed from human sense.

Does the past make sense to a child? A successful historian has to know a lot. Sue Wilcock reminded me that teachers will need help with this. They will not (often) know the history in sufficient detail and we need to keep the thinking and subject knowledge required simple. We all, however, trip up. I recently got caught out by a student asking me – 'so who was king in 1934? Was it George the V? Edward the VIII?' I couldn't remember. But then again, I am not connected with royalty, I am the sort of historian who would rather know what people had for breakfast in 1934. I suppose I am a bit like the children in the interviews below and Joanne Philpott's students. I need history to make human sense. The question 'Who are the English?' is about making a connection with people in the deep past and is about the big story of the people. And we must not forget the children in these interviews – they did understand and have a feeling for what was being asked of them. So, I think, do teachers, but like the Year 5s and 6s they are just a little less confident that they know the 'right' answer and this makes them a little more reluctant to tell.

The case study

This project sought to develop four ways of teaching the full implications of our inheritance. Research was through:

- a discussion forum – to identify what children already thought and knew about our people history
- An ideas trial – to try out 'new' ideas for a history week.

Children's historical understanding and thinking often surprises me because once I am able to free them from the notion that I am searching for the right answer they reveal amazing insights into the past. In preparation for this chapter I interviewed children in a number of schools. I remember a KS 2 child at Sedbergh Primary School who told me about Ptolomy and Cleopatra, even though he had never studied the Egyptians at school. During previous research KS1 children at St Mary's, Kirkby Lonsdale (in 2003) were able to tell me about the people who lived here after the 'Ice Age' (yes they knew about it before the Walt Disney film) and how they lived in huts, cooked on a fire and got their water from a river. These were not interview questions. These were replies from children who had been encouraged to talk about what they knew about certain times in the past.

Forum methodology
Questions were given to small groups of pupils in Years 3, 4 and 6 who, after discussion, wrote their own answers and thoughts on a big sheet of cloth – a metaphor for making thoughts permanent because they were indelible (and writing on cloth felt slightly naughty). They did their own writing but each statement was always agreed by other members of the group.

To remind them of the history they knew already, interesting objects and pictures (relating to early British history) were placed in front of them. These were: Roman pottery, a model of a Stone Age hut and some coins.

They could ask questions about the objects and pictures but the discussion was theirs.

Forum results: so who did the children think lived here before us?

The replies from the children at Tatham Fells School near Lancaster were no less fascinating than the examples of children's existing knowledge above. I wanted to know whether the children could connect themselves to the peoples who once lived here who were not English. A similar question might be asked in Scotland, Wales and Ireland.

The questions put before the children in the Ideas forum were:

- What was it like here before it was England?
- What language did we speak before English?

At Tatham Fells, the question 'What language did we speak before English?' strikes deep at our peoples' history. There was confusion of course, I was interested that none of them said Latin (although the Year 4s wrote Italian), one group of Year 5s said American (they also talked about German as a possibility), but the brave Year 3s said Welsh and Welsh people might have lived in England.

Fantastic, because after a little bit of digging the children identified the Welsh as Celts. Thus with German, Latin (Italian) and Celtic we had covered three of the roots of English.

Their vision of the pre-English past was equally interesting because there was a lot of talk of cavemen, Vikings and Romans. Some identified cavemen as being Stone Age (but were still resolute in their belief they lived in caves – which they did not). There was plenty of talk about animal skins for clothes, fires for cooking, and stones and bones for tools. Interestingly, one group was unsure about whether cavemen could talk.

Finally, I asked a group of Year 6s if they could produce a time-line of all the peoples they had discussed. They put 'people' at one end and 'cavemen' at the other. Then along the line they placed Stone Age, Bronze Age, Romans, Vikings, Saxons and Tudors all in the correct order. Well done them!

At St Mary's the discussion was different and seemed less successful at the time. However, the ideas presented concluded that the ancestors were Villains, Scottish, Vikings, Romans, Saxons, Celts, Cavemen (who were Stone Age) Greeks and finally, French (the Normans). As before, the children seemed surprised that their ancestors were not English but were readily able to supply a mostly plausible list of who they might be. As for the idea of what language was spoken, the children gave a lesser response, but identified Norse (Norwegian) Latin (Italian) French, Native language, Greek, grunting and even English as possibilities. The brackets indicate some confusion on their part.

Exploring these ideas and values during a week with the theme, who am I?

During the week we developed a range of practical ideas to develop the cross-curricular theme. These will need to be re-adapted to suit your own class and here they are presented as developed for able children. These activities are discussed in more detail below and included:

- playing with and mathematically investigating time in a way which allows pupils to relate the passing of time to their own ancestry. This activity will also allow them to follow the real development of human ideas through history (the time line linked with mathematics)
- investigating locality to see the influence of the invaders and settlers on the landscape (place names linked with geography)
- following the development of English as a language and engaging themselves in translations of some of the earliest written sources on England (translating languages, English and literacy)
- and, finally, find out what's in that envelope.

Reinventing the historical time-line with help from mathematics

Dawson (2008) talks about the curriculum in terms of 'thematic stories' and, like Philpott (2008), he talks about this book as a block to a child's chronological understanding. Such a story is often lost when we teach through discrete periods of history such as the Romans or the Vikings in the National Curriculum. He likes the idea of a thematic story because it tells us that what we are learning is a construct or interpretation of the evidence. His most enticing point is that we do not teach the big picture and he argues that we should get the pupils to tell the stories themselves and that the pupils should be able to link the themes to events today.

Dawson's argument is a useful one for those teaching history at KS2 and it is perhaps one for the teacher to answer first. Can I tell the 'thematic story' here? And perhaps even more crucially, can I tell the big story, the one about how 'those people's' lives link to our own? We have all been told countless times about the value of the humble time-line. Wicked historians such as myself ask how will we know who came first, the Vikings, Saxons or the Romans, unless we use a time line? We need to make this humble instrument work harder, for it can help us to see the interconnectedness of history. For only then can we see that there are not English but Mesolithic settlers, Romans, Moors, Celts, Saxons, Vikings, Scottish, Irish, and so on.

Stow (2005), in summarizing thinking on values in history teaching, points out that an explicit value of the teaching of history has been to, 'inculcate children with certain values and attitudes'. Traditional teaching of history, he goes on to say, will, among other things, equip a child with a corpus of historical facts. The facts, he goes on to remind us, can be used to tell many stories (my word) and that the story (particularly in these times) depends on the values of the teacher, the prevailing politics and even the values of the school/management. He also notes that teaching, resources and displays can make the experiences in history of other cultural groups irrelevant or non-existent. This is fundamental to this project because in order to understand the interconnectedness of cultures and history it is necessary to make the time-line able to connect Britain to Greek science, Roman writing and Babylonian mathematics. We might, for example, connect a trivial event such as the development of the pencil to the advent of written communication in Mesopotamia some 5,000 years before.

Mathematical time-scrolls

True understanding of the interconnectedness of all things and the peoples' real history requires pupils to be able to follow events across vast tracts of time. This concept is explored with the pupils as the idea of a 'time-scroll'.

This task can be reinvented and stretched to fit the needs of your own pupils, as it stands it is work undertaken by an able group of Year 5s and 6s on their own.

The group's task was to reinvent the time-line as a 'time-scroll' (a piece of wall-lining paper which could be wound up) using mathematics and history. Britain has been importing ideas and undergoing a process of civilization since some time after 5000 BC. Therefore, the first time-line covered 7,000 years and was extended by a further 4,000 years later in the week. The group had to measure time through the scroll using three number systems; dates, years ago (BP) and numbers of ancestors.

Ancestors are important as they help the child place themselves in time. This can be calculated by dividing the total number of years by 22 – an approximation of the number of years per generation (you might more easily and justifiably use the number 20). (We had a long discussion about this word; a generation is the average time gap between being born and having one's first child.)

It looked like this:

DATE	2007	1000	0	1000	2000	3000	4000	5000
YEARS AGO	0	1000	2000	3000	4000	5000	6000	7000
GENERATIONS	0	45	90	135	180	225	270	315

Only it was quite a lot longer. The top line indicates the date, the BCE dates going backwards caused some head-scratching. The middle line is the number of years ago and the bottom line is the number of generations or ancestors you might have had. I am guessing that the number is far smaller than you might have supposed. This last is the important number because it makes history nearer than one might think, almost the whole of the important bits of our people history is covered in just over 300 generations.

Back to McGuinn (2002) and his reminder for us of Prometheus' quest for forbidden knowledge and his stealing of fire from heaven. We can use the time-scroll with other groups to show the 'fundamental interconnectedness of all things'. By using the time-scroll we might link Prometheus' fire to the discovery of metallurgy in the Near East and the Industrial Revolution in Britain.

A time-scroll allows us to add lines to ask and answer questions about the past. For instance, if we wanted to find out about all the developments in human history that have had to take place all over the world in order for us to be able to produce a packet of 'Wheat O's', we would need to

1 Take a careful look at the product and the packaging and decide all the inventions that have led to us being able to make it.
2 These might be wheat itself. A type of wheat known as einkorn was first farmed in Mesopotamia, an area now known as Syria, in about 9000 BC. So the arrow for wheat will go back to before our time-line begins. On the way along the arrow other significant events will be picked up such as when wheat was first grown in Britain (after 5000 BC).
3 English writing on the packet: Mesopotamians seem to have invented writing sometime around 3500 BC. The Phoenicians invented an alphabet on which ours is based around 1000 BC. The Romans first brought writing to Britain in AD 43. The English language may have started to appear around AD 500. All these events would be marked along the written English arrow.

English – translating Caesar

Bryson (1990) in his book *Mother Tongue* reminds 'us' that 'English' can be heard in the lands beyond Schleswig-Holstein when people ask 'What ist de clock?' This area was once called Angln and was the home of the Angles. I found the same thing when walking through a forest in Sweden with my friend Svante, asking him the names of the trees, ek (oak), alm (elm), björk (birch) and found that they were not so very different from our own.

In the past I have asked pupils to make their own 'English is a Foreign Language Anyway' dictionary. I used a Swedish dictionary (but you might as easily use a Danish or Norwegian one) to show the links with the Norse language. Here are some of the words we tried:

- finger
- snow
- freeze
- bread
- law
- house
- sister.

We simply looked these English words up in the Swedish dictionary to see if they were similar in spelling and meaning. The key to under-standing this is that words change over time, therefore sister is syster and so needed a bit of hunting because i had changed to y (a short dictionary works best). Our dictionary contained notes on how the word was pronounced and any differences in meaning. But our language does not only come from the Saxons and Vikings. You could also use a Latin dictionary to do the same with the so-called romance vocabulary:

- violence
- trepidation
- tepid
- suspend
- suspicious
- stagnant
- ridiculous
- pest
- onerous
- fix
- dissolve
- denude
- curator
- bonus
- arm.

Britanniae pars *interior* ab eis incolitur quos natos in *insula* ipsi *memoria* proditum dicunt, *maritima* pars ab eis, qui praedae ac belli inferendi *causa* ex *Belgio* transierunt (qui omnes fere eis nominibus *civitatum* appellantur, quibus orti ex civitatibus eo pervenerunt) et bello illato ibi *permanserunt* atque *agros* colere coeperunt.

The groups often got a sense of the translation below within 7–10 words.
The interior part of Britain is inhabited by those of whom memory says were born in the island itself. The coastal areas, by those who had come from the country of the Belgae for the cause of plunder and making war. Almost all are called by the names of the places from which they came. And having waged war, they stayed and began to cultivate the land.

Figure 3.1 Annotating a Latin extract

Pupils who worked with the Latin from Caesar's *Gallic Wars Book 5* were encouraged to draw circles and lines over any of the words that they thought might have been similar in English. They were then encouraged to use an English/Latin dictionary to work out more of the words. As they worked they began to form a sense of what Caesar was writing about and as soon as they felt confident they were encouraged to produce their own 'translation'. There was some excitement about who had produced the closest match.

Understanding that English is a synthesis of other languages is central to this project. Being able to draw on original sources and use them is the act of a historian. Using Caesar in Latin you may regard as a step too far, but it works and some of the pupils mentioned that they felt they had done some real history. This is, of course, the type of activity that can be differentiated, less able groups might translate the words of Pepys, on the 7th June 1665 he wrote:

> 'I did in Drury Lane see two or three houses marked with a red cross upon the doors, and "Lord have mercy upon us" writ there; which was a sad sight to me, being the first of the kind that, to my remembrance I ever saw.' (http://pepysdiary.com)

which demonstrates how our language changes, or the words of Bede on the invaders and settlers:

> *Book I, chapter 15* – ... Those who came over were of the three most powerful nations of Germany – Saxons, Angles, and Jutes. From the Jutes are descended the people, of Kent, and of the Isle of Wight, including those in the province of the West-Saxons who are to this day called Jutes, seated opposite to the Isle of Wight. From the Saxons, that is, the country which is now called Old Saxony, came the East-Saxons, the South-Saxons, and the West-Saxons. From the Angles, that is, the country which is called Angulus, and which is said, from that time, to have remained desert to this day, between the provinces of the Jutes and the Saxons,

Short directory of place names; based on de la Mor La Souriete (1997) which is easily available on the web.

Celtic and Prehistory:

- **Bre and Penn:** words for hill
- **Dun:** also meaning hill
- **Ced:** meaning wood
- **Kumb:** meaning valley

Latin:

- **Egles:** church
- **Wic:** vicus
- **Camp:** campus
- **Ceaster:** which actually comes from the Latin castra meaning fort

Saxon:

- **Folc:** folk
- **Burh:** fortified place
- **Stoc:** place, farmstead or hamlet
- **Tun:** enclosure, farmstead, village, manor, estate
- **Ham:** homestead, village, manor, estate
- **Brycg:** bridge belonging to the estate or manor
- **Mere:** pool by the dwelling or farm
- **Lea:** wood, woodland clearing or glade, later pasture
- **Eg:** island, land partially surrounded by water, dry ground in a marsh

Norse:

- **Thorp:** farm or hamlet
- **By:** village
- **Ingle:** English
- **Ir:** Irish
- **When:** 'of the women'
- **Kirby:** church
- **Wath:** ford
- **Holme:** island, dry ground in marsh, water-meadow
- **Ulpha:** hill where there are wolves
- **Stan:** stone

Figure 3.2 Place name suffixes to support the activity

are descended the East-Angles, the Midland-Angles, the Mercians, all the race of the Northumbrians, that is, of those nations that dwell on the north side of the river Humber, and the other nations of the Angles ... (http://www.heorot.dk/bede-caedmon.html)

Geography, a new take on an old activity, place boxes
In a useful and readable digest, de la Mor la Souriete (1997) points out that English place names come from a variety of languages – Celtic,

Pre-Celtic, Latin, Old English, Old Norse and Norman French. Just think of all the places in Yorkshire and Lincolnshire with names ending in 'by' or 'thorpe' which are both Norse (Viking) words indicating settlements. This matters, the names of our towns are precious and part of our culture, and yet many were named by incomers.

I have tried two ways to enable children to identify these patterns of place names. The first is by placing a perspex sheet over a map and writing place-name translations on it using a whiteboard marker. The second is to make place boxes. How do our towns and villages reveal traces of those who lived and settled here in the past?

- Children look at a map of the locality and make lists of place names which have similar 'bits' (suffixes) at the ends. They write them on small boxes.
- They explore the meanings of the suffixes (against the list on page 45) and place them in the boxes.
- They do the same with the prefixes.
- As soon as they are able to translate a whole place name (try Kirkby) they write it on a new box, with the full translation inside. Note – I encourage more able groups to use de la Mor la Souriete's fuller list to gain a better understanding of the meaning. It will not be possible to translate all elements of place names.

Concluding the week

At the beginning of the week you will recall that each group was given an envelope containing a task which could be opened on Thursday. This task would provide a way of summarizing children's findings in different ways. It is targeted at different abilities and aptitudes:

- Group 1. Write a poem about 'the people who arrived'.
- Group 2. Write a ghost story about 'the spirits of the people' who remain.
- Group 3. Write a poem and song about my 'forgotten ancestors'.
- Group 4. Produce a PowerPoint or video documentary about 'the settlers'.

Conclusion

When I asked my students 'Why study history?' the answer was almost always an emphatic, 'So we can learn the lessons of history'. Reading Cicero on the political machinations of Rome in the time of Caesar, or Bede's tirade against the Saxons, there is only one lesson that history teaches us – we do not learn the lessons of history.

So why teach or learn about history? Because we learn about ourselves, about where we come from and, most of all, for me at least, about the fascinating lives of those who lived before me – lives which more than anything make my own seem more bearable. It is also, to paraphrase Herodotus, to preserve from decay the remembrance of what men have done and prevent the great and wonderful actions of the Greeks and the Barbarians from losing their glory. (From the Story of Io).

This classroom project was about identity, diversity and understanding the global dimension of our small lives through time. It is understanding that this country is what it is because of, to quote my son Joe, 'the evolution of the peoples' and because nothing, not our language, our towns and cities, our roads, the way we farm the things we farm, our industry, our thinking or even simply telling the time are purely British. This is not about stealing our soul either because we can all be proud that this historical fusion of ideas and cultures that occurred here – to 'us' – has affected world history.

By bringing together history, geography, mathematics and English we have enabled history to be both rigorous in its own right at the same time as contributing to the understanding of three other subjects.

References

Bryson, B. (1990) *Mother Tongue*. London: Penguin.

Dawson, I. (2008) *Teaching History 130*. June. London: Historical Association.

De la Mor la Souriete, C. (1997) *A Survey of the History of English Placenames*. Available at www.eng.villages.co.uk/vill-names.html. (Accessed 4 December 2008.)

Donaldson, M. (1985) *Children's Minds*. London: Flamingo.

Fullinwider, R. (2006) 'Multicultural education', in R. Curren (ed.), *A Companion to the Philosophy of Education*. Oxford: Blackwell. pp. 487–500.

Grosvenor, I. (1997) *Assimilating Identities, Racism and Educational Policy in Post 1945 Britain*. London: Lawrence and Wishart.

McGuinn, N. (2002) 'How and why do we Learn?', in I. Davies, I. Gregory and N. McGuinn (eds), *Key Debates in Education*. London: Continuum. pp. 29–41.

Philpott, J. (2008) *Teaching History 131*. June. London: Historical Association.

Pryor, F. (2004) *Britain BC*. London: Harper Perennial. pp. 32 and 158.

Richards, J. (2001) *The Blood of the Vikings*. London: Hodder and Stoughton.

Stow, W. (2005) 'History: values in the diversity of human experience', in R. Bailey (ed.), *Teaching Values and Citizenship across the curriculum*. Reprint. Oxford: Routledge Falmer. pp. 67–89.

Valuing my place: How can collaborative work between geography and art help make the usual become unusual?

Chris Barlow and Andrea Brook, with contributions from Dawn Shuttleworth and Paul Bowden

Art week was cool, really relaxed, I got to make an acrylic painting of my part of the village with Chas Jacobs and the walk down to the sea was brilliant – my painting is on the wall in the hall, come and have a look. (Molly Forrest, 10 years, Saint Luke's Primary School)

Chapter introduction

Every day children trudge to and from school through the seasonal delights cast by typical British weather: same people, same place, same footpaths, same streets. It is very easy therefore to forget that this place is unique, that this place is always changing and that for children this place is 'their' place and their place is special.

This chapter uses this idea to consider how teachers can help children to look again at the normal everyday locality of their school. What new treasures can be found? How can the norm be made more interesting? How can the usual be made far more unusual? How, as Williamson and Hart (2004) suggest, can the 'ordinary' be made 'extraordinary'? How can teachers help children examine their own place through different eyes?

Children are active learners from birth, making sense of their multi-sensory environment ... as teachers we can plan activities

(Continued)

(Continued)

to help pupils question and understand their surroundings. (Hoodless et al., 2003: 136)

The following case study attempts to inspire and support those of you who seek opportunities to raise the profile of geography within the school, to empower colleagues, to connect with the school environment, to raise standards through more active and engaging learning, while offering the children in your care something perhaps more relevant, exciting and fun.

Geography

Geography is an all-encompassing discipline, with endless potential for both meaning and enjoyment in learning. As geography is all about people, places and environments, it permeates into every area of our lives and to every area of learning – a definite curriculum 'jewel' (Geographical Association, 2007). Yet Ofsted remain concerned about the national profile of the subject. 'Geography continues to have a marginal status in many schools compared with core subjects and those foundation subjects which are perceived to have greater priority' (Ofsted, 2005).

Current trends towards greater school ownership of the curriculum could prove to be of advantage to geography. As many schools move towards a more thematic approach, the purpose and place of geography is again up for discussion within the curriculum. 'Geography teaching and learning should be an enjoyable, creative and magical experience for pupils and teachers alike' (Richardson, 2007).

Geography and values

In primary schools where geography is taught outstandingly well and where it is promoted by subject leaders and senior managers, the subject is seen as adding valuable breadth and richness to the curriculum. (Bell, 2007)

Geography learning opportunity is important to the development of young minds. It builds upon the child's own experiences to widen learning horizons, meeting new people and places along that journey. As children progress they develop a solid skill base for life, allowing exploration to be successful. Geography offers the chance to both understand and appreciate the world, to become socially responsible citizens, with views formed from well-balanced experiences. Through

The children discussed likes and dislikes in their community

geography children learn to recognize their place in an ever-changing world.

The Geographical Association Primary Position Statement (2007) identifies the following geography learning opportunities:

- stimulate children's interest in their surroundings and in the variety of human and physical conditions on the earth's surface
- foster children's sense of wonder at the beauty of the world around them
- help children to develop an informed concern about the quality of the environment and the future of the human habitat and thereby enhance children's sense of responsibility for the care of the Earth and its people.

> Geography makes a major contribution to children's physical, intellectual, social and emotional development. In short, geography matters. (Geography Association, 2007)

No other subject offers the opportunity to relate issues directly to your own life and to the lives of those around you, while also exploring the world at a variety of levels. When taught well, geography offers perennial fascination to the individual, nurturing 'everyday geographers', for we are, as Fran Martin (2006) suggests, sharing something of great value with them that will help them to 'live in the world'.

Perhaps, like the introduction of the National Curriculum, which was at the time considered to have put the subject of geography clearly 'on the map', recent curriculum changes in the light of *Excellence and Enjoyment* (DfES/QCA, 2003) allow dedicated teachers and concerned school managers to take advantage of greater ownership of subjects through thematic and creative approaches, which may well finally give geography the chance to truly shine. 'Teachers have much more freedom than they often realise to design the timetable and decide what and how they teach. Other ways of finding time for geography include theme days, clubs, school councils, extended projects and research' (Geography Association, 2007).

Cross-curricular geography

Essential to any consideration of a more thematic or cross-curricular approach towards curriculum opportunity is the idea that one theme may offer wide opportunities for quality learning in several subject areas, thus supposedly saving time and repetition, while allowing for wider and more cohesive learning experiences, with greater consideration of how children learn. A number of studies have identified the extent to which children relate closely to cross-curricular approaches due to an apparent preference for more holistic learning. These are discussed further in Hoodless et al. (2003) and in Barnes (2007).

Geography can conceivably link in a purposeful way to all subjects. This is, however, dependent upon teachers being able to recognize both the essential nature of each subject, as well as recognizing the pedagogical 'good practice' that may be encountered. In many schools, as Ofsted recognizes, the use of effective school subject management is critical to such development. The recent trend towards a more cautious thematic approach is arguably not the 'full circle return to topics' that some of my older colleagues have suggested, but is, I believe, a direct move away from the tenuous links that topic web planning *could* encourage, to a far more balanced, child-centred and responsible curriculum vision that favours creativity, innovation and true cross-curricularity.

The case study offered in this chapter is an example of one school's attempt to explore greater geographical opportunity in a more cross-curricular way, by seeking valuable shared learning experiences in the local community, with art.

The case study

Saint Luke's Church of England Primary School lies 2 miles north of Lancaster, in the small leafy location of Slyne with Hest. A short walk from the school gates takes you through woods and fields, to Lancaster Canal, towards breathtaking views over Morecambe Bay. In this sleepy location, Tudor and Victorian buildings sit side by side with the bungalows of suburbia, while quiet country lanes lead you to tennis courts, the children's playground, the bowling green and the church.

A recent Ofsted inspection recognizes the high quality of learning on offer. Praise is given to the dedication of all staff and the willingness of the school to reach out and embrace the contribution that the wider school community and the locality can offer. The school seeks ways in which curriculum entitlement in all areas can be enhanced, providing exciting and meaningful opportunities for all.

Every year in May this forward-thinking village school takes a break from the 'normal' curriculum, while 'Art Week' takes over.

This themed week is a time for opportunity, creative thought, individual expression and lots of fun! The Office for Standards in Education increasingly endorse and trust the autonomy of schools in managing the curriculum in a far more stimulating way, recognizing both the varied ways in which children learn, and the dedication of innovative hard-working professionals. 'If you're not careful school can get so result minded; it would be great to have times built into the year when the focus is all about enjoying the process and trying new things out' (David Atkinson, Deputy Head Teacher, Saint Luke's Primary School).

The idea of such curriculum enrichment weeks is nothing new. Science Week, Poetry Week and Healthy Week are common practice, yet recent governmental educational strategy has empowered schools to actively seek such wider opportunities, rooted securely in the good curriculum practice that such events can offer.

> The difference in approach often sparks children's interests in a way that a set standard lesson presented in a similar way does not – it tends to be far more real and thus connects to some of the 'hard to reach' groups and inspiring them to find out and learn more about the world in which they live. (Paul Bowden, Head teacher, Saint Luke's Primary School)

Celebrating our place

The aim of the week was to embrace the Art Week opportunity, but also as a vehicle for a wide variety of geographical experiences, using the child's own locality as the stimulus for exciting experiences in both subject areas. 'The local built environment, the buildings, places and spaces around any school, is rich with opportunities to motivate, inspire and challenge children's ideas about what they know, think and aspire to' (Williamson and Hart, 2004: 4).

A geographical theme was chosen for several reasons:

- newly appointed school management were keen to reach out and involve the wider school community
- opportunity to celebrate the child's own place and explore the environment on the doorstep, embracing fieldwork in *all* age groups
- new geography subject leader recognizing the need to generate interest in the subject and to raise the geography profile throughout the school
- recognition of creative experiences that would be both relevant and fun for the children
- enthusiastic art subject leader, ready to both manage and offer support to all concerned.

A sense of place

Developing a sense of the child's own place is essential to children's development of geographical understanding. Not only does the study of the local area allow development of essential skills, it also allows for a solid sense of identity and community belonging to prosper. Joicey, writing in 1986, suggested that for children to observe the fine detail of their locality and to learn through 'seeing', would help them to 'understand better the world around them and, through that experience, to understand better the world within them' (Joicey, 1986: 94).

Such learning in turn may then act as a springboard to further investigation, offering a comparative case study from which to explore the wider world. From such firm value foundations of curiosity, empathy and appreciation, children can consider their own attitudes as well as their roles and responsibilities as members of society. 'Children and young people develop their understanding of their role as citizens within local and global contexts and extend their knowledge of the wider world ... they realise the importance of taking action and how this can improve the world for future generations' (DfES/QCA, 2005: 5).

Geography and art

Geography and art work well together, with many shared desirable outcomes. Like geography, art is about thinking creatively, solving problems, working co-operatively, and developing observant and curious young people. While having discrete skills, and knowledge, it allows for divergent thinking and the development of confidence and empathy across the curriculum. According to the National Curriculum for art and design, it provides 'a unique way of understanding and responding to the world'. As such it is an excellent subject to link with geography, to engage children with the key values of that subject, as well as its own. Thus, when children address such concepts as 'concern for the environment', 'valuing places' and 'awe and wonder', art can be a way of responding to the ideas, through working with practical materials to represent and develop them. 'Developing a sense of your environment involves observing and talking about its main character-istics, becoming articulate about what you like (or dislike) about it, maybe recording it in drawings, plans and models' (QCA, 2000, in Cooper, 2004: 96). With thoughtful planning, art can become the vehicle through which children show their understanding and present their findings in geography, while developing the skills and knowledge of the art curriculum.

Art and representations of place

Whether or not it is through poetry writing, map-making, model-building, songwriting, poster design, drama or story, a sense of place can be explored in many creative ways, allowing children the opportunity to investigate and express their views, feelings and understanding through a variety of stimuli, from a variety of voices. Figure 4.1 suggests artists who represent place in many different ways.

Art offers many approaches towards the representation of place which, when harnessed, can be of great interest to the geographer:

* How have famous artists represented *their* place?
* How would they represent *our* place?
* What views in our locality do you think Van Gogh or Monet might have chosen if they had lived here for a while?
* How would our streets look to Lowry?
* How might our locality have influenced the designs of William Morris?
* What would a Breughel celebration scene look like set in our village?
* Could we represent our place through sculpture?
* Are there any artists who have been inspired by our locality?
* Do we have any artistic talent within the wider school community?
* In what ways would we like to represent our place?
* Are there approaches we would like to explore that we have never tried?

Useful websites to explore specific artists' representations of place can be found at WL 4.1–4.7.

Fieldwork opportunity

During Art Week the opportunity to experience the child's own loca-tion through fieldwork was given high priority (Figure 4.2).

Fieldwork in the local area, including exploration of the school buildings and grounds, is essential to good practice in primary geography and hap-pens every time you leave the classroom door with some preconceived

- The Boyle family – 'Journey to the Surface of the Earth'
- Pieter Brueghel
- Gerald Cains
- Cezanne
- Brian Cook
- Patrick Cullen
- Ray Evans
- Manet
- Claude Monet
- Simon Patterson – personalized maps
- Henri Rousseau
- Seurat
- Philip Wilson Steer

Why not try representing 'your' place in an artistic style from history … e.g.:

- Bayeaux tapestry style
- Chinese willow pattern style
- Eqyptian style
- Roman mosaic style

Examine sketchbooks of artists who travelled to see how they recorded the environment
e.g.: Paul Gaugin, Victoria Crowe – use these to inspire your own sketchbooks of the local area

Figure 4.1   Other artists with a strong sense of place

investigative purpose in mind. Good geography provision recognizes the immense positive contribution that such opportunities can offer children, and seeks to overcome such potential barriers as organization, risk assessment and time constraints, in favour of the rewards of skill development, social interaction, enquiry learning, 'hands on' memorable and meaningful experiences, and the huge potential for enjoyment through collaborative learning. 'Fieldwork is of central importance to geography. In terms of learning to live in the world, it is the main means by which we can learn to make sense of what we see around us – the landscapes in which we live, work and play' (Martin, 2006: 26).

In addition, participation in fieldwork is statutory to the requirements of the geography National Curriculum for both primary key stages. Children should, 'carry out fieldwork investigations outside the classroom' as well as use fieldwork skills and techniques' (DfEE/QCA, 1999: 16).

According to Richardson (in Scoffham, 2004: 135) the 'magic of going out' is of particular interest when applied to the child's own locality. Raikes (1991), cited in Cooper (2004: 11) recognizes that 'the immediate environment is a wealthy source on which adults can draw if they are prepared to do so'. The children on this occasion are the experts and can certainly teach their teacher a thing or two. Children know the best places for secret dens, the hidden special places, the local

	RECEPTION	YEAR 1	YEAR 2
	Celebrating Our Place **Art Week Timetable**		
MONDAY		Pastel drawings of an area of the village	'Houses' Feltmaking Gillian Ferguson – Local Textile Artist
	Locality walk – down to the shore	What can we see from our school grounds? – Sketch books	
TUESDAY	Village model making	Village 'Bear Hunt' walk	Locality walk
	Lunchtime 'BIG Environmental ART' challenge – sculptures on the field and playground using natural materials		
	In the Style of an Artist	Textiles work relating to the story 'We're Going on a Bear Hunt' Mrs Gardner	Pastel drawings of an area of the village
WEDNESDAY	Pastel drawings of an area of the village	In the style of an Artist	SCHOOL VISIT Fleetwood – compare and contrast with Slyne with Hest – collect images of this place
THURSDAY	Painting – Village Maps	Water Colour Canal Landcapes Canal Visit	Creative representations of Fleetwood and Slyne
	Dance/Drama/Art activities Jo Barlow	Mrs Sharples	
FRIDAY	Dance/Drama/Art activities Jo Barlow	Drawings of houses from the village and making a class wall map Mrs Sharples	Canal Art Painting with Mrs Layzell
	Painting – Village Maps		

(Continued)

Figure 4.2   *(Continued)*

Celebrating Our Place
Art Week Timetable

	YEAR 3	YEAR 4	YEAR 5	YEAR 6
MONDAY	Locality walk	Locality walk	SLYNE MANOR Whole class painting Mrs. Pilkington	Chas Jacobs Local artist will be working with Year 6 in small groups through-out the week.
	In the Style of an Artist - Seurat	Art Showcase Students from Beaumont college to show art work. (Mrs. Davidson~ Pennington)		Locality Walk
TUESDAY	Pastel drawings of an area of the village		Locality walk	In the Style of an Artist
	Lunchtime 'BIG Environmental ART' challenge – sculptures on the field and playground using natural materials			
	Village Environmental Audit	Pastel drawings of an area of the village	In the Style of an Artist - Lowery	What Can we see from our school grounds? – Sketch books
WEDNESDAY		Workshop with Chas Jacobs Local Artist	Views Across the Bay Feltmaking Working with Gillian Ferguson Local textile artist	Environmental art on the shore. Chris Barlow
	Our Village Workshop with Chas Jacobs Local Artist	In the Style of an Artist		
THURSDAY		3D models of local buildings in the style of Hundertwasser Andrea Brook	Pastel drawings of an area of the village	
	Painting and pattern work from 'Google Earth' images Mr. Connolly		Canal Art Paintings Mrs. Layzell	
FRIDAY	Village Board Game Design Chris Barlow	Chalk big map of the village Chris Barlow		
	Village Board Game Design Chris Barlow			Pastel drawings of an area of the village

Note: names of visitors to school who offered to run sessions are shown underneath the relevant activity

Figure 4.2   Celebrating Our Place: timetable of the week's events

names for places and their own personal connections – all areas of great value that a cursory stroll during a teacher's planning and preparation time, simply cannot hope to recognize. 'This prior knowledge is priceless and can be tapped into and channelled into further learning opportunity through use of "a structured pathway"' (Paula Richardson, in Scoffham, 2004: 135).

Children hold strong views with regard to the quality of their environment. From a very early age likes and dislikes, 'good' and 'bad', what is held precious and what they would like to change can be explored. In addition, they may not make connections between people's actions and the quality of the environment, and so work exploring their place can be of infinite societal value as well as of great variety and interest. The local environment is a 'rich learning resource full of clues about our past, who we are and how we got here; and it is a challenge for the future: how we want to live and who we want to be' (Williamson and Hart, 2004: 3).

Perhaps the primary aged child I witnessed recently, riding his bicycle too fast on the pavement, before throwing an empty drinks can over his shoulder into the garden of an elderly local resident, would think first about his actions if geography had offered him an opportunity to explore his environment from a variety of different perspectives and to value the place in which he and others live.

Art Week: celebrating our place

> The kids loved art week, there were so many different things to do. (Alison Jones, parent governor, Saint Luke's Primary School)

As you can see (Figure 4.2) the opportunities on offer during the week were extensive.Much thought was given to the content and quality of the five available days. At the early planning stage it became clear that four goals were essential:

- a wide variety of opportunity beyond the scope of the 'normal' prescribed school curriculum
- to welcome the wider school community, as experts and as willing support
- to offer quality geography and art experiences
- excitement, enjoyment and achievement for all.

> *In art week you never know what's coming – but it will be good.* (Lauren Pilkington, 10 years, Saint Luke's Primary School)

The week began with an introductory assembly on the theme of 'celebration'. This introduction, recognizing the unique nature of every school community, helped to focus children's minds on what was going to happen during the week ahead. In addition, it helped nurture a sense of collective purpose and relevance. Children had been briefed the Friday before, so many model buildings had arrived that morning ready to contribute to the big map idea on the Friday.

The structure of the week had been carefully managed by the subject leader for art, in negotiation with the geography subject leader and school management. Allocations of opportunities were carefully distributed throughout the school. Each class teacher had been offered guidance and individual staff ideas assimilated. The views of children had been considered through the School Council and events had been negotiated and explained in whole-school staff meeting time.

The variety of opportunity on offer included:

- sessions with local artist Chas Jacobs, famous for his blue skies and balloons (later continuing his friendship with the school to paint the entire library with Year 6 children)
- work inspired by established artists
- work inspired by more contemporary artists such as Andy Goldsworthy and Friedensreich Hundertwasser
- location-specific art styles such as canal art.

Example activities

Foundation Stage: We live by the sea
As the village is close to the sea, a parent volunteer offered to explore a multi-sensory approach to representing the nature of this environment.

1 On the first day of Art Week all the children visited the shore. They thought what it would be like and what clothes would be appropriate, and they talked about what they thought they might see there. When they arrived at the shore they collected materials they had talked about; what they could smell, hear and see. They collected different textures and considered different colours, shapes and patterns. They asked questions about what they had found. They observed that there were many sticks and bottles and pieces of wood that were high up on the bank – they wondered if the sea was always so calm – they considered what it would be like in the winter when the wind brings big waves and there are black clouds and a storm. They noticed that some of the bank was falling into the sea and wondered if large waves must sometimes crash into the soil. They noticed shells and pebbles and seaweed, wood, plastic, feathers and an old shoe – they wondered why some of these objects were found so high up on the shore away from the sea.

   - They looked at how people used this area.
   - They wondered which animals might call this place home.

A creative look at the bay

- They talked about what they liked and disliked about this place.
- They shared experiences of visiting similar places.
- They took photographs of different things that they could see.
- They thought of good words to describe this place.
- They wondered what it would be like to live on the shore.

On return to the classroom this fieldwork experience was used as a stimulus for a series of approaches exploring the seashore theme. The children recalled the things that they had seen at the beach. Some of the objects found were passed around and the children looked at pictures they had taken. They talked about beaches that they had visited – other pictures were used to help stimulate interest.

2 Children looked at the pictures they had taken and then listened to sea-inspired music – they noticed how the music changed as the sea moved towards a storm. Musical instruments were then used to re-create the action of the sea – calm, up and down waves, rough sea, stormy sea, waves crashing, thunder and lightening, crescendo, and back down to peace.

3 Children listened to the simple story of 'The Starfish and the Boy'. This introduced the idea that they could make small differences to their own environment through small positive actions.

4 Children re-created 'the Starfish and the Boy' story using sand, sparkly material (sea), pebbles and toy sea creatures – children represented the characters in the story – physical involvement through movement and discussion of meaning.

5 The idea was now introduced that this environment can change and that some of the items on the shore and the way in which the bank was worn away happen when there are big storms. Classical and modern images of storms were introduced and discussed.

6 The storm images were then used to allow children to express their own version of a storm on canvas squares, using thick paint, glitter, sponges, thin paint, blowing straws, brushes, fingers, and so on. Children listened to the sea music again while working.

7 Children made their own design ideas for salt dough starfish.

8 Children painted large beach pebbles – while working they were encouraged to tell the story of each pebble – where has it been? What has it seen? How does it feel? How old are they? What colours might be best to represent the pebble's story?

9 Sand pictures were created, using the fieldwork experience as a stimulus for patterns, shapes and images.

10 At the end of the session the parent introduced the idea of the speaking pebble. Here children took it in turns to hold a large 'special' pebble – when they have the pebble they were encouraged to say a statement about why the shore at Hest Bank is special.

> It was a magical day, the children were so focused, I think the step-by-step approach really helped to immerse them in the idea of living near the sea shore. They had lots to say and the depth and variety of their ideas were amazing – it was incredibly rewarding to be involved. (Joanne Barlow, parent)

> It was a really interesting experience, as I was not the leader on this occasion I could sit back a little and watch the children trying out each activity – I could make observations regarding their participation and achievement which I used to inform my record-keeping. (Glynnis Cunningham, class teacher, Saint Luke's Primary School)

The children's work during this session was later displayed for Open Evening, using collage seaweed handprints, fabric collage and sand pictures, creating a really imaginative display that the children were very proud of.

Further work using the Percy the Park Keeper story 'After the Storm' and the 'big book' *Barnaby Bear Visits the Seaside*, expanded the themes explored during Art Week to less familiar locations.

Year 3: Game design
In this class 7- and 8-year-old children, were given the task of evaluating the environmental quality of their locality and then using this information

Board games set in the village of Slyne with Hest

to inform game designs, based on their likes and dislikes about their environment.

This activity aimed to develop children's local area enquiry skills, while promoting values of community spirit, appreciation, consequences of actions, consideration of the effects of change and the benefits of learning together. The local area setting meant that children on this occasion were definitely the experts.

The process:

1 Environmental enquiry: exploration, observation, recording and discussion of likes and dislikes. Children considered how their area could be improved.
2 Children worked in groups to discuss their findings. They created lists of positive and negative observations: they considered the causes and consequences of each set of statements.
3 Introduction of the board-game idea. How does a board game work? What is successful? What do they look like? How are they decorated? Children examined a variety of games and used this research to inform their planning.
4 Children asked to consider how the points that they have raised could be incorporated into a game that would help encourage people to treat *their* place with more care and respect.

5 Planning time was given to consider layout, content and 'look' of the game.
6 Games were completed.
7 Games were tried out with classmates and other age groups and, finally, with parents at Open Night.

This idea took longer than expected, such was the nature of the preparation and the time needed to produce work that the children were proud of. Working in small mixed-ability groups helped them to formalize the ideas that visiting the local area had generated.

It was fascinating to listen to conversations where children discussed their environmental outrage and pride through the inclusion of 'move forward', 'roll again', 'go back to the start' and other board-game value conventions. 'That's where the shop is, if you land on that square it means you picked up some litter, so you can move forward four spaces' (Melissa Lindsay, aged 8, Saint Luke's School).

Once the children were familiar with the snakes and ladders style game format, the urgency to create took over. It became clear early on that the children wanted their games to be played rather than just created, and so in their eyes they had to be good. Such motivation helped develop the artistic approach towards their work, as careful design choices had to be made with regard to colour, composition, shape and general visual appeal. If people wanted to play their games they would actually understand how the village could be improved. This was ultimately very rewarding; the children's ideas were well conceived and the care and attention to detail was admirable, indeed the idea of a game set in *their* place proved an irresistible 'hook' to achievement for all. 'Using local geography as a resource to support learning in other curriculum areas is a fantastic way to motivate pupils because the learning is real, relevant and exciting' (Owen, 2007: 12).

Year 4: Using a less familiar artist – Friedensreich Hundertwasser

> We made models of buildings in our village. We could totally change them and add different colours and patterns – I added stripes and towers. It would be great if things were really like that … it would be like living in a dream. (Max Molinari, aged 9, Saint Luke's Primary School)

Using the architecture of Friedensreich Hundertwasser is an exciting way of linking the work of an artist to a topic on the environment: it meant that the class of Year 4 children could use their drawings from their walk around the local village both as a stimulus for three-dimensional (3D) model-making, and as a chance to embed their knowledge of the artist's ways of working.

A village make-over – Hundertwasser style

Hundertwasser was an Austrian artist and architect. His work is well known in his own country, particularly in his quirky, easily recognizable buildings. These illustrate his philosophy as an environmentalist, and relate to his experiences both in his own country and the rest of the world – in New Zealand there is even a Hundertwasser public toilet!

In the classroom, looking at posters of Hundertwasser's work encouraged lots of discussion on identifying the kinds of images, colours and patterns the artist used in his artworks and buildings. There were several large posters in the classroom, as well as a variety of postcards on desks, and the children were able to identify different symbols used by the artist and discuss why they thought he had used them – as well as why his buildings appeared to have rather wobbly horizontals, not to mention trees appearing to be planted in unusual places! They took a little time to make sketches of the shapes, recording the colours, and then had to imagine how they might construct their own model building, if they were to take on the persona of Hundertwasser. This led to excitement and further discussion, and the children were shown the variety of materials available in the classroom to support their constructions. (These were chiefly collage materials – collections of coloured papers and fabrics, differently sized boxes, feathers, and other collected items). The children had brought the boxes from home during the preceding weeks and they had placed them on their tables, looking at them from all angles, and discussing in their groups how they might create their building – and then decorate it.

Teamwork was essential – lots of discussion led to basic construction, using initial sketches for inspiration and the boxes collected. Later in the morning the painting began, with thickly mixed paints, using the information gained from the children's Hundertwasser studies. ('How about purple here, light green there … ?' 'Yeah, and yellow there!' 'Is that OK – an orange door?' 'Oh yes!' 'How do you mix black?') Keiran became the natural leader of his group of three, telling them which colours to mix; he also protected areas of his group's model with paper towels so that the colours did not run. In the afternoon the children were able to choose the special 'extras' to add to their buildings. These had been kept at the front of the class and one child per group was sent out by each group to gather a small collection to add touches to their models.

Working over a whole day was very satisfying – it meant that the children could remain focused on one task, able to see the fruits of their labours at the end of the day. It also meant that the organization of the classroom could be disrupted for this contained period, without worries of clearing away for the afternoon! (If this amount of time were not available, working over several weeks could also have positive outcomes – with children able to think about the next stage of their models during the week, perhaps planning with their group and getting ideas from the models of other groups – as well as looking more closely at the work of Hundertwasser). Of course, the need for an organizational strategy was paramount and it was a great advantage that the children knew how to access the classroom materials in a calm and confident manner, and could therefore concentrate on their activities with the minimum of disruption.

An artist whose work is closely linked with Hundertwasser is the Spanish architect Gaudi, whose buildings so inspired the later artist in his use of colour and pattern. Other artists/architects might have been used for reference – Lowry's work fits well if a northern urban landscape is under investigation – 'How has it changed? Why were houses built in this way?' are questions which might be asked in relation to this artist's work. More contemporary architects might also be investigated – the work of Norman Foster, changing the face of London, for example. Or the teacher might discuss why buildings look the way they do – and how they have changed over time.

As well as encouraging co-operative skills and creative problem-solving, this kind of work can help children to empathize and to understand that there are different ways of seeing the world and representing/creating it. The form and function of buildings could also be investigated both locally and in the wider world; and in the present or the past. Although geography is an immediate link, there is also opportunity to link with history, drama, science and design and technology (D&T). Working with the

Stone spiral

artist Hundertwasser invariably engages children – from Foundation Stage upwards – and creating buildings is just one possible route to 'using' the artist. An examination of his work can lead to a variety of other artistic responses – collage work; creating symbols for different subjects; print-making. The list could go on.

Year 6 environmental art
On the Friday of Art Week, 36 Year 6 children donned Wellington boots and waterproof jackets, to head for the shore at Hest Bank. The aim of this session was to combine natural materials with shoreline flotsam, to create exciting environmental sculpture art inspired by the work of artist Andy Goldsworthy.

Andy Goldsworthy is a northern sculptor, photographer and environmentalist. His work draws on the character of the environment, and uses natural and 'found' objects to create amazing pieces of sculpture. Andy's work is large, tactile, awe inspiring and thought provoking. In my experience children respond very well to this accessible and less traditional approach to artwork.

Prior to the fieldwork session the children had been introduced to Andy's unique way of representing the environment – they examined a selection of his work and they expressed their views regarding his particular style. Through discussion and use of describing words and annotated images, they examined composition, use of materials and

Collecting materials on the shore

the variety of shape and texture. In addition they searched for any meanings in his designs and considered his own motivations and his possible attitude towards his environment. 'I think he likes space and freedom, he likes to be outside and do what he wants to do' (Catherine Elley, 10 years old, Saint Luke's Primary School). 'I think he likes nature, but likes to surprise people who pass by' (Jack Tanner, 11 years, Saint Luke's Primary School).

When the time came to visit the shore the children were both excited and well prepared for the opportunity to create their own ideas inspired by his work. They were ready to look at the local area anew and apply what Martin describes as 'geographical imagination' (Martin, 2006: 30).

The session began with a short sensory exploration. Children were then asked to work in small groups to explore their initial feelings and existing familiarity with the shore. They wrote words describing their feelings for this location in the sand and gravel. These activities gave children the time to fully connect with the outside learning environment and to consider the 'canvas' that they would be using.

We took time to listen to the silence and considered why this place is special. The children considered what might interest Andy Goldsworthy if he was with us, what potential would he see in this location?

As most children were already familiar with this location, it was important to establish early that we were looking at it in a different way and

Hard at work on 'Twiggy Breeze'

that there is much this place may offer us. It was important that they respond to a stimulus in their own ways within a simple structure to allow the imagination of young minds to flow.

For this activity to be successful the school had to think carefully about risk assessment; however, the visit was planned for a time when the tide was low, protective plastic gloves were worn and health and safety points were discussed with the children. Despite an intermittent chill wind the children did not stop all day, moving from each challenge with energetic enthusiasm. 'It was really good fun, it wasn't like being at school at all' (Alice Tidswell, aged 10, Saint Luke's Primary School). 'Amazing, they concentrated for so long' (Denise Hines, parent helper).

During their day on the shore many activities were introduced – each task added to the 'gallery', moving along the shore as the children's creations accumulated.

1 Treasure hunt – as a warm-up activity the children were asked, in groups, to create a resource pallet by collecting a variety of natural and human-made objects that they might be able to use in their work. This included pebble piles of different sizes, colours and shapes, feathers, driftwood, plastic bottles, rope, netting and shells – the activity helped children to familiarize themselves with the location as well as to consider the possible use of different objects.

2 Introductions – children were asked to create their name using the materials they have just collected.
3 Sacred spirals – children created spiral designs from pebbles and shells.
4 Lines – cross-hatch line designs using driftwood, rope, string, grasses and sticks.
5 Mosaic – children composed a mosaic pattern in any ways they thought represented this place. 'We placed collections of feathers in each corner because the bay is famous for all the birdlife.'
6 Museums and towers – during lunch children were encouraged to create 'matchbox museums'. The challenge was to include as many different items as possible, while also creating pebble towers – arranging the pebbles in ways they thought were pleasing to the eye.
7 Arches – having examined arches in Andy Goldsworthy's designs, the children had a go at making their own – a real 'group' organizational challenge.
8 Sacred stones – children created sacred pebble and found object circles.
9 3D fun – using found materials children created their own three-dimensional sculpture.
10 Challenge time: tall sculpture – children were given the task of creating the final part of our sculpture trail – a walk through sculpture isle – each sculpture had to represent this place and had to be as tall as I am.

> We made 'Twiggy Breeze'; it represents what can be found on the shore. It's made from driftwood and is decorated with shells and pebbles. The grass and string hang down from the branches and catch the wind – it's very windy here. (Calum Kyle, II.)

Through this work the children were encouraged to connect with their environment, to see it as a valuable resource, a place of inspiration and wonder – a place to value, respect and, hopefully, cherish.

Final thoughts

> The aims, ideas and content of primary geography have a clear outcome in mind: the informed, concerned and responsible member of the community. (Catling, in Carter, 1998: 41)

This chapter has offered you the opportunity to consider how geographical themes can be combined with other subjects and how the everyday environment around your school location can be revisited and transformed into something wholly more exciting, interesting and unusual.

> Local studies provide an excellent opportunity to present learning in a manner which is meaningful to primary children, and which will therefore interest and

motivate them. It is through the study of the local environment that many disciplines meet and converge. (Hoodless et al., 2003: 55)

For children, local area investigation can, through combination with a visually sensitive subject such as art, help children, as Barnes (2002) suggests, to become 'awake' to the appearance of their surrounding world.

Looking at the 'known' through different perspectives gives children the opportunity to value their place and the community to which they belong and to realize that it is unique, special and interesting. Engagement with their local environment throughout the primary phase of learning can reinforce this notion and can result in long-lasting values such as belonging, societal ownership and social responsibility, and pride in 'your' place. Such attitudes of interest and stewardship will be transferable to studies of more distant places *and* to choices made in life. So perhaps such work offers children a sharpened visual and emotional sense, and an ability to see with greater insight, as observed by Barnes (2002).

> I think that many of the children enjoyed art week because it linked strongly with their emotions, they were proud of their achievements and they had the opportunity to express how they felt about things in their community. (Dawn Shuttleworth, art subject leader, Saint Luke's Primary School)

Through such work children can closely engage with their own very individual environment, having the opportunity not only to explore the known in a new and exciting way, but also to consider what they value in their community and how they could actively work towards improving and sustaining the very nature of that place ... and who knows, it may also be fun!

Planning considerations

Wonderful as it may seem to children and parents, successful management of such cross-curricular breaks from the norm often mask great amounts of preparation. With the involvement of parents and the wider school community, the use of fieldwork and more adventurous timetabling, there are many areas to consider. Careful planning is essential so as not to create managerial chaos and to ensure that the resultant 'buzz' of creativity is both purposeful and enjoyable for *all* concerned.

Planning process

- Senior management team meeting with art and geography leaders, and members of University of Cumbria to discuss the potential of this idea.

- Staff meeting to launch the idea – bring the team on side – opportunity to revise the content of good art and good geography – ideas discussed.
- Opportunities for wider school involvement explored – letters to parents, newsletter, phone calls made, contacts sought – offers considered and managed by subject leaders and allocated to appropriate classes.
- Further planning meeting to discuss final content of the week and to agree shared opportunities and assessment.
- Logistics of staffing, resource implications discussed.
- Timetable of events and other relevant information disseminated at staff meeting.
- Subject leaders offer support and advice to staff members prior to Art Week.
- Art Week begins with a whole-school assembly exploring the theme of 'Celebrating our place'.
- Art Week closes with a walk round each class to view completed work and a celebratory assembly.
- Examples of work created are displayed two weeks later during Open Night.
- Review of Art Week undertaken by subject leaders.

Critical factors for success

- Out of the box thinking – start with a blank page and let your minds wander.
- Early collective planning.
- Shared ownership from within the school – commitment of all concerned.
- Dedicated support from school management.
- Financial commitment to resource purchasing.
- Resources easily available during the week.
- Well-managed timetable.
- Clear communication between all involved.
- Clear leadership from subject specialists.
- Opportunity to experiment and reflect on the success of approaches used – time for curriculum bravery and risk-taking.
- Recognition of the professionalism of each individual within the school.
- Clear communication to parents.
- Opportunity for the wider school community to become involved at a variety of levels.
- Opportunity to celebrate achievement.
- Children involved in the planning process.

- That the essential nature of both subjects was revisited and maintained.
- That the wider social benefits were recognized.

Although achievement during this time was displayed in a Summer term open evening, focus during the week was always on process rather than outcome. This allowed the children to relax into a variety of challenges, which in turn allowed experimentation and creative thought.

Bibliography

Bailey, R. (2000) *Teaching Values and Citizenship Across the Curriculum*. London: Routledge and Falmer.

Barnes, J. (2007) *Cross-Curricular Learning 3–14*. London: Sage.

Barnes, R. (2002) *Teaching Art to Young Children*. London and New York: Routledge/ Falmer.

Bell, D. (2007) *HMI: Geographical Association Primary Position Statement*. Sheffield: Geographical Association.

Carter, R. (ed.) (1998) *Handbook of Primary Geography*. Sheffield: Geographical Association.

Cooper, H. (ed.) (2004) *Exploring Time and Place Through Play*. London: David Fulton.

Cox, S. (ed.) (2007) *Teaching Art & Design 3–11*. London: Continuum.

Department for Education and Employment/Qualifications and Curriculum Authority (DfEE/QCA) (1999) *The National Curriculum for England. Geography*. London: QCA.

Department for Education and Skills/Qualifications and Curriculum Authority (DfES/QCA) (2003) *Excellence and Enjoyment: A Strategy for Primary Schools*. London: QCA.

Department for Education and Skills/Qualifications and Curriculum Authority (DfES/QCA) (2005) *Developing the Global Dimension in the School Curriculum*. London: QCA.

Geographical Association (2007) Primary Position Statement. www.geography.org.uk/ eyprimary/positionstatement/

Hoodless, P., Bermingham, S., McCreery, E. and Bowen, P. (2003) *Teaching Humanities in Primary Schools*. Exeter: Learning Matters.

Joicey, H.B. (1986) *An Eye on the Environment*. London: Bell and Hyman.

Martin, F. (2006) *Teaching Geography in Primary Schools. Learning to Live in the World*. Cambridge: Chris Kington.

Office for Standards in Education (Ofsted) (2005) *Geography Subject Report*. London: Ofsted.

Owen, P. (2007) 'Why fieldwork matters to every child: *Primary Geographer*, Summer: 12–14.

Richardson, P. (2007) in D. Bell, Geographical Association Primary Position Statement. Sheffield: Geographical Association.

Rowley, C. and Lewis, L. (2003) *Thinking on the Edge*. Kendal: Morecambe Bay Partnership/Living Earth.

Scoffham, S. (ed.) (2004) *Primary Geography Handbook*. Sheffield: Geographical Association.

Tickle, L. (ed.) (1996) *Understanding Art in Primary Schools*. London and New York: Routledge.

Williamson, C. and Hart, A. (2004) *Neighbourhood Journeys*. London: Cabe Education.

Journals

Primary Geography – Geographical Association (www.geography.org.uk):

- Autumn 2005 Valuing Places
- Summer 2006 Cross-curricular Approaches
- Summer 2007 Learning in the Outdoors

5

Learning to value another place: promoting cross-curricular learning with geography and ICT through a local school link

Rob Wheatley

Chapter introduction

In this chapter Rob Wheatley of the University of Cumbria and Anna Copping and Lisa Read at Marion Richardson School, Stepney, work with children over a week linked to a visit to Leigh-on-Sea. The work over one week links geography with ICT and history. In the concluding task, children imagine what Southend might be like In 2050. Taking Barnes's (2007) notion of 'powerful experiences', this work looks at the importance of such an experience in promoting both good cross-curricular practice and more authentic experience of place. Materials have been created showing how spreadsheets might be used in environmental surveys. Children used desktop publishing to create work booklets on the topic of how shops have changed in a local centre over the past 50 years. This was linked to the creation of a shopping database. PowerPoint was used to show the benefits of talking books.

The early years of the twenty-first century have proved to be difficult for primary geography. The 2005 annual Ofsted subject report labelled geography as the 'worst taught subject' in the primary curriculum. Although geography has been by no means alone in this criticism, The Geographical Association responded with its action plan for geography, designed to reinvigorate the subject at primary and secondary level. A key aspect of this has been to encourage a clearer focus on key geographical concepts. In the summer of 2006 a project was developed with a Year 5 class of a local school in Bethnal Green to study the village of Theydon Bois in Essex. The village is only 30 minutes away by underground but is in a rural setting and contrasts with the children's home area. Contact was made with the village school in Theydon Bois and arrangements were made for their Year 5 class to host a visit from the Bethnal Green School during our field trip. This proved popular with both Year 5 classes, with the Bethnal Green children saying this was their favourite part of the day. During the rest of the day children took digital photographs around the village, drew sketches and collected traffic data. Upon their return to school they were then given two weeks to prepare a PowerPoint presentation explaining the differences between Bethnal Green and Theydon Bois.

This was supported by secondary data on such topics as housing, employment and travel to work. The group returned to the village school and the children presented their PowerPoint presentations to the Theydon Bois children. Results were impressive, with the children creating presentations using the main features of the programme and identifying key geographical differences between the two locations. Having experienced the enjoyment the children gained from their geographical work, a decision was made to develop a similar project but based on a nearby coastal location.

Leigh-on-Sea

As with the field trip to Theydon Bois, it was felt important to have a contrasting locality but one that was easy to reach by public transport. The town of Leigh-on-Sea lies on the north bank of the Thames estuary, some 30 miles from London, within the borough of Southend-on-Sea. It has a long history, appearing in the Domesday Book and growing as a port in the Middle Ages, benefiting from trade with Europe. During Tudor and Stuart times shipbuilding was well established but, due to a rise in sea level during the eighteenth century, the deep water channel became silted up and shipbuilding declined. Fishing, especially for shellfish, remained an important local industry. The mid-nineteenth century saw the coming of the railways and the town was well located to appeal to tourists from London. Tourism still plays a major role in the economy of the town. This part of Essex, however, suffered badly from flooding in the early 1950s, which affected the tourist trade for some time. Since the mid-twentieth century the north bank of the Thames estuary has been home to large-scale industrial sites such as the Ford Motor factory at Dagenham and the oil refineries of Canvey

Island. In contrast to this industry, the area also has its own nature reserve, Two Tree Island, and the estuary is an important ecological asset. The town lies in the proposed Thames Gateway development, which covers both banks of the estuary down river from London. The largest wind farm yet proposed in the UK lies to the south and east of the town. In summary it is a town that has seen its industrial fortunes change because of environmental change. How might children envisage the future for Leigh-on-Sea?

Geographical concepts, places and values

In this chapter I focus on children's concepts of the future and their development of values and place attachment in connection with that. It was hoped that a project could be developed that would allow children to explore their own values and those of others in the context of futures. The notion of the insider/outsider perception of place could also be explored to see if they had an impact on values. Finally, some consideration of the value that children attach to particular places would also be undertaken.

Concurrent research for an MPhil/PhD had led to consideration of a number of ideas linked to place and the development of values. Hicks (2007) identifies the need for a futures dimension in the curriculum. He considers the idea of preferable and probable futures.

Futures and values

Hicks (2007) points out that there is a lack of agreement on the type of future that people want, differences deriving from age, gender, class and culture. He goes on to say that there is often a tendency among young people to feel either change is not their responsibility or that they personally can make little difference. 'To do nothing, however, is to assent to the status quo, and the question "What part can I play here?" lies at the heart of citizenship' (Hicks, 2007: 184).

Futures, it seems, offers a fertile area for values education. Hicks further identifies the idea of the 200-year present:

> in many communities there will be people who were born a hundred years ago. In talking with and listening to such members of the community we are linked through their life experiences with the events of the last hundred years. Similarly there will be babies born today who will live for a hundred years. Maybe this is the period of time for which we should feel some sense of temporal responsibility since we are rooted within it. (Hicks, 2007: 184)

Wiegand (1992) recalls the work of Relph (1976) who suggested that we experience places as either insiders or outsiders.

Values and the idea of insider and outsider perspectives on place

> To be an insider is to have deep personal knowledge of a place and to experience a sense of belonging. Being an outsider means viewing places in a colder, more detached way. But within each of these two forms of experiencing places are levels of intensity, according to the degree of emotional involvement we might feel towards places. (Wiegand, 1992: 32)

He then subdivides insiders and outsiders into seven categories based on these degrees of emotional involvement. It would be interesting to see if pupil perception of the future was influenced by their insider or outsider status.

Place attachments

Finally there is the idea of place attachment. Martin (2006: 150) refers to the work of Spencer (2004) in recognizing that adults can recall details of places that were important in childhood. He quotes other research that shows how children and adolescents take 'ownership' of and develop emotional attachments to places.

Organizing the project

The Tower Hamlets School that volunteered to take part in the project was the Marion Richardson Primary school. The school has 490 pupils on its roll, is situated just off the Commercial Road in Stepney and last year celebrated its centenary. The school population reflects the variety of minority ethnic communities living in Tower Hamlets. The project was to be undertaken by two Year 5 classes. Both class teachers, Anna Copping and Lisa Read, were newly qualified teachers (NQTs). The two classes also have a support teacher, Noireen Sullivan, who has worked at the school for many years.

At an initial meeting with the three teachers the aims and organization of the project were discussed. I undertook to prepare a draft scheme of work and collect resources that would support the project. Information was collected from various websites (WL 5.1–5.20) about the town, future developments such as the Thames Gateway and the London Array wind farm. Information on population, employment and housing types was gained from the UK census. A half-hour regional television programme about the town was located on the Internet and Pathé newsreel clips of the 1950s floods were downloaded from the London Grid for Learning website. A collection of digital photographs was also begun, to supplement any that the children took during the visit. The collected information was then used to create a variety of fact sheets to support the children's learning. These covered topics on history, the future, and the environment and industry.

Imagine it is the year 2050. You will be 53. You have received an email from a friend who lives in Australia. They and their family are coming to visit London but their parents were from Leigh-on-Sea and they want to visit the town. Do you know anything about the town? You have to create a PowerPoint that:

- Gives a little history of Leigh
- Says what it was like in 2008
- Says what it is like in 2050

Figure 5.1 The task set

The draft fact sheets (WM 5.1 to 5.5) were then reviewed by the school staff to ensure they were written at a level that the children would be able to access. In order to provide a structure for the children's work they were provided with a brief for their PowerPoint presentations (Figure 5.1).

In addition the children were given the following questions to think about:

Has Leigh changed for better or worse?
Why did the changes happen?
Could it be different?
Do you think people like living in Leigh in 2050?
Why might different people have different views about the town in 2050?

All these questions draw on the work of Hicks (2007). I was interested in establishing whether the children had an optimistic or pessimistic view of the future and whether they felt they could influence future, events in any way or that the future is decided by other people. Some exploration of their values with regard to the environment would also, hopefully, be explored. In addition I wanted to see if, with only a brief visit and a week working on the project, they might have developed any form of attachment to Leigh.

A preliminary visit was undertaken in late May. For the school staff this was their first visit to Leigh and they were keen to gain a sense of the town and to reassure themselves about safety issues. Three sites were chosen for the children to experience different aspects of the town. The amount of time to travel between locations and possible sheltering points were identified.

Finally, to prepare the children for the visit, time was set aside for me to give a small presentation about the project to both classes. The structure of the final PowerPoint presentation was explained to them and they were given the chance to ask questions about the visit and the project in general. They also had the chance to view the television programme about Leigh. This was a useful step as it meant the children knew something of the town before they visited and had an idea of the things they might want to look out for when they arrived in the town.

The visit

The journey

In hindsight, the first Monday after a half-term was perhaps not the best possible day for a school trip, but it was the only available date, so 60 children and eight adults set off from Limehouse station on the 30-minute journey to Leigh-on-Sea. During the train journey the staff tried to signal the changes through the train window such as the change from residential London to the industrial landscape along the Thames estuary, the transition to the low-lying mixture of agricultural and marshland, the looming presence of the oil refinery at Canvey Island and, finally, the coastal landscape of Leigh itself. The children had been divided into three groups for the day and, within each group, into smaller groups of three who would work together to produce the final PowerPoint presentations.

In Leigh

Because we knew that the children had seen the video about Leigh-on-Sea and that we had fact sheets prepared to support their work on a variety of topics, the aim of the trip was to allow them to experience the town through as many of their senses as possible. The recording information was kept to a minimum and an emphasis was placed on talking to the group about the location and clarifying any misconceptions.

Overview of the town

The first location was chosen because it gave a view over the old town of the harbour, nature reserve, oil refinery and across the Thames to Kent. We reminded the children of the video they had seen and asked them what they recognized. The well-known 'cockle sheds' where the produce of the local fishing boats are processed, was the most common answer. Children were asked to choose a view to sketch and to take photographs with a digital camera provided for each group of three. This would later be used in their PowerPoint presentations. While they were working, staff drew attention to and explained the various features in view. The children expressed enjoyment at seeing the range of boats in the harbour and surprise at the low-lying nature reserve on Two Tree Island only just above sea level.

The old town

From here the children were divided into the three groups to walk through the old town of Leigh. Each group was given a different location which had contrasting building styles. Once again the children were asked to sketch and take photographs. The adults pointed out interesting houses and building materials, and tried to give some chronology of the old town through its buildings. The importance of the railway became apparent to the children, with frequent trains passing in close proximity to the area.

The beach

For lunch we had arranged for the groups to meet on the small beach at Leigh. Without a doubt, for most of the children this was the highlight of the trip. Having finished their lunch and despite a gentle drizzle, 60 children enjoyed the pleasure of a sandy beach in the way only children know how. For an hour they dug holes, buried each other, defied the waves and searched for shells. Barnes (2007) stresses the need for such 'Powerful experiences'. He suggests:

> Children (and probably most of us) learn most easily through actually being physically involved in exploring sites, materials and ideas. It is incumbent upon schools to produce the most positive and personally productive learning outcomes for each individual. (Barnes, 2007: 200)

Talking to the children on the train home, reading the poems they created and while viewing their PowerPoint presentations, it became clear that the beach would be the trigger memory that would allow them to reflect on their day in Leigh-on-Sea. A powerful experience does not have to involve a trip somewhere. The use of performance artists in school could provide an equally strong trigger. However, when trying to explain the geography of an area and establish connections between things children see, hear, feel, smell and touch, surely visiting the location is a vital experience?

Two Tree Island nature reserve

The final location was on the edge of the nature reserve on Two Tree Island; the plan to go further into the reserve was discarded due to weather conditions. The children were asked to just sit quietly and think what they could see, hear, smell and feel. The variety of flora and fauna was pointed out and the peacefulness of the location was compared to the old town and to Stepney. The change in the state of the tide from high tide in the morning to low tide in the early afternoon was discussed, with large expanses of mud flats now exposed. The return trip to Limehouse saw the children back in school for the end of the school day.

I can see leaves rustling in the breeze
I can smell fresh air in the playground
I can hear voices echoing from buildings
I can see flowers moving with the wind
I can smell petrol coming from roads
I can hear sirens coming from police cars
I can see rocks surrounding a water fountain
I can smell leaves blowing on the ground
I can hear birds singing on the trees

STEPNEY!!!

Figure 5.2 Sound and smell

Creating the presentations

Starting with the senses and links to language

For the rest of the week the classes were going to work on their presentations as much as possible. Some timetable commitments such as swimming, fencing and music had to be kept to, but the rest of the week was made available to complete the project. In the previous week both classes had thought about the sights, sounds and smells of Stepney and had created poems. The same approach was taken to Leigh-on-Sea. It was felt this was a good way to get the class to think about their first impressions of Leigh. Working with one group who were writing down ideas for their poems, they remembered the smell of ice cream and the feeling of sand in their shoes. They remembered the sight of all the small boats on the water, the smell of fish from the fish co-operative and the sounds of the seagulls and the waves. Another child remembered that the houses were different from those in Stepney, 'colourful like Ballamory'. The class teacher, Lisa, took the chance to remind them that they were trying to put an image into the mind of the reader. She asked them to remember the devices they might use, such as rhyme, simile, metaphor, alliteration and onomatopoeia. Figures 5.2 and 5.3 are examples of the Stepney and Leigh poems.

Developing ICT skills

Once the poems were completed, work began on the PowerPoint presentations. Both classes worked in mixed-ability groups. The aim was to produce two or three slides about the past, the present and the future. The children had a range of experience using PowerPoint. For her first computer session with the children, Anna decided that a recap on the process would be useful. Stress was laid on the importance of the text as the aim was to convey information. Once the text was entered, the

In Leigh-on-Sea, the place beyond
Where the sea goes on and on
Where the lighthouse is far away
To see the flowers sway each way.

Where the tides go in and out
The seaweed and shell go all about
When the sound is soft as a feather
The wind touches place in the weather.

After the boats spread all around
Then there's a silence of no sound
Once the cockle shells are in the sheds
The working men go to bed.

The next day they go to sea
Maybe one day they'll even take me
Then the boats start to move ahead
Towards the nature reserve the boats were red.

All the buildings were old and new
It makes the buildings have a different varied view
So many things in Leigh-on-Sea
So many places for you and me

Figure 5.3 Leigh-on-Sea

children would then select images for the presentation, either their own digital photographs, photographs from the project collection or from the Internet. Anna reminded them how to select slide styles. Work on formatting the presentations would take place later in the week, when the children would consider backgrounds and slide transitions.

Anna was pleased with the opportunity that group work gave the class to co-operate and work as a team. They had to negotiate over the inclusion of text, selection of pictures and sequence of slides. Talking to the class while they were working it was clear that they understood the task and had a good grasp of the information they wanted to convey about Leigh in the past and present.

Back to the future

It was decided to tackle the idea of Leigh-on-Sea in the future after having a discussion with the classes. I began by telling them some of my own experience of change. I had first moved to East London about 20 years ago to teach in a school not far from Marion Richardson. Many of the class were very surprised that one of the features of the local landscape, Canary Wharf, was not there. I explained that the Docklands Light Railway had also not been constructed.

They were then asked to say if they thought people would like living in Leigh-on-Sea in 2050 and which groups of people might benefit from that. Much of their thinking centred on the issue of flooding. During the week the idea of global warming had been mentioned several times by children. Time was taken to explain the theory of global warming. It was explained that people held different views on the subject, namely, that some people think it is not happening and some people think it is happening but that there is nothing we can do. Others think it is happening but there are steps that can be taken to reduce its effects. The future for the town in the eyes of most children lay in their opinion about global warming. During the discussion a range of views was voiced. One group thought that the town might add a new tourist attraction that would bring money to the town which could be used to strengthen sea defences. Others felt that it would not be possible to stop the flooding and the railway line which runs along the coast would be in particular danger. Many felt that the fishing industry also faced a difficult future mainly due to overfishing, or, because of global warming, a change in the species of fish in the estuary. Once the class had had the opportunity to share their views then they finished their presentations.

The presentations

In all, 16 presentations were created. It was pleasing to see the use of maps to help describe the location of Leigh. Geographical vocabulary was also evident with terms such as 'coastal', 'mudflats' and 'development' featuring. All the groups made the distinction between the old and new town. The children included their own digital photographs that they had taken during the visit and supplemented them with photographs from the Internet. Of the 16 presentations, 10 took a negative view of the future for Leigh, suggesting that due to global warming the town was in danger of flooding. Four took a positive view, suggesting that the town would prosper. Two groups set out both the positive and negative futures but did not say which they felt was more likely. Generally the Thames Gateway project was seen as positive, bringing homes and jobs to the area. The building of the wind farm was also seen as positive. Many presentations suggested that the fishing industry might have a difficult future.

There is evidence here to support the ideas of Hicks (2007) and possible futures. In the last opinion the use of 'might' suggests that the group does not have a fixed idea of the future and they can see that a range of things may happen. However, because they have had to speculate, they are trying to draw upon the knowledge they already have and apply it to a new situation. This would seem to be drawing on the skills of analysis and synthesis taking children beyond description. Secondly, the idea that new species may be a

> 'The sun will make the sea really hot and the sea will make the fish really hot as well and we won't have any more fish to fry'
> 'There will be less fish and Leigh-on-Sea might not be a fishing town anymore'
> 'The fish that Leigh-on-Sea has now will go and different species will come to the sea. It might be a bad thing that different species come to the sea because they might not be edible'

Figure 5.4 Children's perspectives on the future of Leigh

bad thing once again leaves open the possibility that it might not be. I believe this to be a powerful strategy in getting children to think about the connections that we aim to study in geography. However, they do need practise in order to develop their analysing and synthesizing skills.

An interesting point refers back to Wiegand's idea of insiders and outsiders. Many children seemed to hold the notion that Leigh-on-Sea was in some ways separate, that the town would need to build a wind farm to generate its electricity; they did not recognize that we have a national energy system. While they expressed attachment to the town and said they would like to visit it again, they did see it as a separate location. Wiegand talked about *existential insiders,* those who know that this is the place where they belong. He also talks about *empathetic insiders* and gives the example of recognizing the specialness of a sacred site without sharing the religious tradition that is associated with that place. It may be that the children were developing a new category to add to Wiegand's list, that of *existential outsider.* The children expressed a liking for the town and were concerned for its future, but they knew they were not part of Leigh.

Children found it hard to see that the issue of global warming might also affect them in London, which is at approximately the same sea level. When the idea was raised that if Leigh suffered from flooding then probably London would too, there were quite a few surprised faces. However, several presentations made suggestions as to how the impact of global warming could be reduced. These focused on reducing the use of private cars, increased use of public transport and switching to renewable energy resources.

What was learnt?

At the end of the project I interviewed eight children and the two class teachers. I first asked the children what they thought they would remember about the week. I was expecting the day trip to be the most popular choice, and indeed several children chose this, but I was quite surprised at how many said that working on the presentations had been memorable.

ICT

The children enjoyed the idea of research and turning it into a finished ICT-based presentation. Once again this idea adds weight to the 'performance of understanding' idea suggested by Barnes (2007). He sees the chance for children to show what they have learnt by presenting it in a new situation. Both teachers also expressed the view that the link to ICT had made the week more interesting for the children. Many schools now have access to digital video cameras and the preparation of a short video would allow children to work in quite large groups, each with a different role in creating the presentation. Showing the presentation in assembly or to parents would add to the power of the event. However such presentations do not have to be ICT based. A drama production based on, 'Leigh-on-Sea, past, present and future' would have been equally valid and may have sparked the interest of a different group of children.

Children's voices

Past, present, future

When asked what they had learnt during the week, the children replied that they had discovered about the past, present and future of Leigh-on-Sea. They had also seen the differences between life in Stepney and life in Leigh. Several children said that thinking about the future had been the hardest part of the project.

Issues raised

Turning to the issue of global warming I asked them what they could do to reduce its impact. They suggested such things as saving energy, car sharing, more use of public transport and making sure computers and lights were switched off when not in use. One child suggested that writing persuasive letters to the government about the need to reduce the use of cars would be possible. When asked what other people or authorities could do, once again the reduction in the use of private transport was the most common answer. New designs for battery-powered cars and an increase in the development of wind farms were also suggestions.

Attitudes and values to place attachment

I next asked them how they would feel if they read in the newspaper in 20 years' time that Leigh-on-Sea had suffered from flooding. Here I was trying to see if they had developed an attachment to the town. Some said that they would think that it was always going to happen. Others said they would be sad because they had memories of the town and really liked it. Several said how much they would like to visit again.

Suggestions for next time

Pupil evaluation

My final question to the children asked them to consider what else could we have done to improve our study if we had more time. Several children suggested it would be good to interview local people about their lives. Extending the visit from just the old town to the new town, it was suggested, would give a better understanding of the town. Visiting a school was also suggested, so they could establish with other children what life in this place was like.

Teacher evaluation

When interviewing the class teachers my first questions asked what they felt the children had learnt during the week. Both Anna and Lisa felt they had begun to learn how to look at a place in a geographical manner. Lisa felt that they would now be able to structure their own investigation. They also pointed to the development of their skills in the use of PowerPoint. They felt the linking of geography and ICT had worked very well. Anna also suggested that it was good to see the use of poetry; it provided a creative outlet and the children saw that it is possible to learn about a subject in ways other than worksheets.

On being asked if they would change anything if repeating the experience, Anna felt that, as they found thinking about the future the hardest part, it would have been useful to include a few more activities during the week that would have allowed them to develop their understanding of the concept. She also felt perhaps a slightly narrower focus would have helped some children as they found it difficult to see the connections between the different things that they observed: homes, employment, transport and environment. Lisa felt that, had it been possible to make the school visit, the children would have come closer to understanding life in Leigh and would have seen how much they had in common with the children there.

I then asked the teachers if they had noticed any difference in response from the classes as compared to a normal week. Anna felt they had been very excited about the trip and also that they had much more access to computers than normal, which they very much enjoyed. Lisa was particularly impressed with one child who she felt had excelled during the week. She had been able to make connections between the things she had seen and offer explanations of her views to other children, something that she had rarely managed before. Both Anna and Lisa felt that the first Monday after a half-term was not ideal for a variety of reasons. Anna felt that she might give the class some more experience of PowerPoint before undertaking the project. They both felt a visit to a local school would have added another dimension to the project. Finally, I asked them if they preferred cross-curricular work in a block such as the week of the project or spread out with a small amount of time each week over the course of a term or half-term. Both felt that the concentrated block of time had its advantages; the children knew they had the week to create their end product.

My own evaluation

Finally, I considered my own views of the week. I would very much have liked to have involved some of my Initial Teacher Education (ITE) students in the project but this was not possible due to teaching practice and lecture commitments. I feel that both the school and the ITE students would have gained from the experience of perhaps 10 students working with the classes. It would have given the students experience of geography in action and it would have given the children greater access to adult support. Losing a visit to the primary school in Southend which we had hoped to arrange was a disappointment. In the previous project this was the most memorable part of the trip for the children. Establishing that life in Leigh-on-Sea had many similarities to life in Power Hole let and that we have shared futures may well have been made easier through children talking to each other. It reinforced my view that the best geography is active geography. It would have been quite possible to complete the study without visiting the town. However, I am sure that the visit provided the motivation for the hard work that we saw through the rest of the week. The importance of fun was also underlined. Having fun on the beach will probably be the abiding memory for most of the children and what will take them back to the town in future years; it played a significant part in their attachment to this place. Barnes's notion of 'powerful experiences' as a fundamental element of cross-curricular learning was certainly demonstrated in this visit.

The need to use geographical vocabulary and to explain the meaning of terms was also reinforced. By the end of the week the children were confident in using geographical terms because all of the teachers involved had used geographical language and taken the time to ensure children understood them. This did not mean, however, that the children did not hold misconceptions. Two examples relate to wind turbines. One child felt that they helped limit global warming because they blew the carbon dioxide away from the area where they were situated. Another child felt it would be a good idea to put turbines all along the beach at Leigh so that if it did flood the turbines would be able to blow the water away. It is only by having conversations about such issues that it is possible to address such misconceptions.

Conclusions

What is it possible to draw from a week's cross-curricular work, which included elements of values education, futures education, place attachment and the idea of how we perceive places as insiders or outsiders? As suggested in Chapter 1, history and geography are subjects that are value laden. Taking a cross-curricular approach to allow children to consider the future of a locality certainly provides a scenario where values and the connection between a variety of issues can be explored in some depth. The idea of using children's perception of the future of a place or a community can offer an opportunity for them to experience values education. While not easy, and something they are perhaps not used to, with careful preparation it does allow them the scope to consider themselves in relation to possible futures. It may also allow them to make the positive step of acting upon their values even if only in a small way.

Values relating to two particular areas were highlighted by the project. The first was children's attitudes towards the environment. The second was explored through the methodology adopted. A high priority was placed on the importance of discussion, negotiation and collaboration. While the children may not have noticed the values that were implicit in the approach adopted, they certainly responded to and enjoyed the process.

Considering the idea of place attachment, choosing a location that was different from their own locality, not too distant, had distinctive features, and somewhere that they could easily visit later in life seems to have provided relevance and motivation. Showing children how easy it is to visit a locality that could be relevant in their later life seems so much more sensible than picking a location simply because the Qualifications and Curriculum Authority (QCA) has already written a medium-term plan for that location. Surely relevance and affection for a location are much more likely to engender the desire to find out about a place than a government stamp of approval.

Finally, let us return to the idea of whether we view places as insiders or outsiders. Certainly the children felt that this place was different from where they lived. In some ways it was special but their perception was that people would live their lives in a different way to them. If we had been able to let the classes meet children from a local school it might have been possible to explore the ideas and lifestyles that united them rather those that divided them. This is an important issue in an era of global concerns. If we cannot explore how lifestyles have a commonality within a region of the UK how can we hope to recognize it at an international level?

References

Barnes, J. (2007) *Cross Curricular Learning 3–14*. London: Sage.

Hicks, D. (2007) 'Lessons for the future: a geographical contribution', *Geography*, 92(3): 179–88.

Martin, F. (2006) *Teaching Geography in Primary Schools*. Cambridge: Chris Kington.

Relph, E. (1976) *Place and Placelessness*. London: Piön.

Spencer, C. (2004) 'Place attachment, place identity and the development of the child's self-identity', in S. Catling and F. Martin (eds), *Researching Primary Geography*. London: Register of Research in Primary Geography.

Weigand, P. (1992) *Places in the Primary School*. London: Routledge.

6

Challenging my preconceived ideas: an alternative to Florence Nightingale for a history-focused cross-curricular theme with RE

Sue Temple, with Lisa MacGregor

Chapter introduction

The whole cultural make-up of Britain is changing, with a significant potential impact on the children currently in schools today. We felt it was important to explore ways to reflect this in the curriculum and help prepare these children for that tomorrow. Many schools in the north-west of England have few children who have multicultural backgrounds. Pupils who live in areas where the majority population is white need to understand that the Britain they see around them is not representative of the whole country. We attempted to broaden the children's understanding and knowledge of different cultures and religions by choosing a project which still fitted under the 'umbrella' of the history curriculum but would help the children understand something of what it means to be a member of a religion they were not familiar with. In addition, we wanted to link to the core subjects of literacy and numeracy. The National Curriculum requires that Key Stage 1 children should study the life of a person who is significant in some way. Florence Nightingale is the usual choice but we wanted to consider alternatives from other cultural and religious backgrounds in order to broaden the range of heroes

(Continued)

(Continued)

and heroines that the children learn about. Many of the famous people children investigate in primary school are male, white and middle class. Noor Inayat Khan did not fall into any of these categories and seemed a good choice. Her life story includes human predicaments, conflicts and difficult decisions made, and therefore would allow the children to begin to understand what is meant by historical interpretations. It is important to avoid presenting a person as totally good, perhaps almost saintly. Children need to understand that we respect real people with human failings who nevertheless lived their lives in an admirable way (Claire, 1996). Jane Mottram, headteacher of Great Corby School, Cumbria, welcomed and supported us in working with staff and pupils of the school.

Choosing the theme and planning

Noor Inayat Khan was brought to our attention in a BBC *Timewatch* documentary which we felt illustrated the potential for a study of her life with primary aged children. Several staff commented that as none of the children had ever heard of her they were all able to start from the same baseline. One teacher commented, 'Everything they found out was new, breaking new ground'. However, this also had disadvantages in finding appropriate resources and information. Another teacher explained 'someone more obvious or well known would have made the research easier'. This shows how important it is to start the planning process in plenty of time to allow for this. Our choice was influenced by a desire to tackle this topic from a cross-curricular viewpoint, exploring the advantages and disadvantages of working alongside religious education (RE), literacy and numeracy. As a Sufi Muslim, Noor met our wish to introduce the children to someone from a different culture and religion as well as to a period in history often covered by the history curriculum. Noor also gave us the potential to include members of the local community, remembering their experiences during the Second World War, helping to involve the whole community, so this was not just a school project that was left at the classroom door. Her experiences as a spy during the Second World War gave scope for including 'spy training' during the week.

Noor Inayat Khan was chosen for a number of reasons. She was: mixed race – American and Indian; a Sufi Muslim; she lived within living memory; and she had an interesting and influential life. In addition, she was

Noor Inayat Khan was born in the Kremlin in 1914. Her great grandfather was a sultan and therefore she was a minor member of the Indian royal family. Noor's father was a Sufi pacifist so she was brought up with these values. Her mother was an American who converted to the Muslim religion. Nazis was brought up in France and fled to England when the Nazis invaded Paris. Noor was an accomplished musician, studied child psychology at the Sorbonne and published children's stories. She joined the Women's Auxiliary Air Force (WAAF) in 1940 and trained as a wireless operator. It was noticed that she had perfect French and so she was invited to train as a spy. In many ways this was against her Sufi principles but she felt strongly against the Nazi regime, so she wanted to support the Allies. Noor was sent to Paris with a life expectancy of six weeks. She was the first woman wireless operator to work in Paris. Noor was able to send vital information back to the British government in London. For many weeks she was their only source of information. She managed to evade capture for almost four months, even refusing to be evacuated because she knew how vital her work was. The Gestapo eventually caught her when she was betrayed by a member of the Resistance. Although she did try to escape on several occasions she later died in Dachau Concentration Camp. Noor was one of only three women who were awarded the George Cross for their services during the Second World War.

Figure 6.1 Background information about Noor Inayat Khan

a princess and a spy (potentially appealing to boys and girls in different ways). Finally, there were clear links with a period of history which is covered in the National Curriculum.

The context and preparation

This project was based in a small rural school in Cumbria with 47 pupils currently on its roll. Although our project focused mainly on the Key Stage 1 class, this project was adopted as a whole-school theme for the week. The Year 1 and 2 children were taught together in the mornings. The Reception children, who were taught with the Nursery children in the mornings, joined them in the afternoons. For this week the teachers discussed the different activities and included the Reception children in those tasks felt to be appropriate for them. The school was keen to try out the idea of a week of activities based around one theme but linked through a variety of curriculum subjects. The project could have been tackled over a much longer period of time and could have been developed in more detail and included further subjects. However, we were keen to avoid tenuous links between subjects and as we focused on planning for just a week, this made us consider and prioritize those activities which were really important to develop the children's skills and understanding. None of the staff was experienced in working in this way, although one or two staff had taught in the 1980s when 'topic' themes were common. In some ways this was an advantage as we were keen to learn from those experiences and find a fresher, more accountable approach, avoiding the tenuous links which were more common then. The whole-school involvement helped to support some of the activities. For example on one day the school kitchen organized a dinner under rationing conditions. As all the staff were included in the planning and drawing up of the timetable for the week, they were able to support each other and generate new ideas through thinking through the project together. A Postgraduate Certificate of Education (PGCE) student on her final block placement was also working in the Key Stage 1 class during this time frame and she felt it had been a tremendously worthwhile experience.

Once we had agreed on Noor Inayat Khan and all the staff involved had researched as much information as they could about her, we were then in a position to start the planning process. Initially we compiled a list of possible activities which would help the children to understand Noor and the decisions she made in her life. We wanted to ensure each activity was valuable in its own right as well as contributing to the overall theme. We then decided which subject areas had the most potential in the classroom and for the intended age group. As it had been agreed that this project would only run for a week we had to prioritize, but other suggested activities are available on the website. We decided to focus mainly on history, religious education, numeracy and literacy with some work linked to other subjects. (WM 6.1 Great Corby Key Stage 1 History Planning Noor Inayat Khan Project June 2008.)

History was the main subject of this project as we agreed that 'History is an umbrella discipline; it involves all aspects of the life of a society – its art, music, science, technology, religion. It lies at the core of humanities and involves children's emotional and social as well as cognitive development' (Cooper, 2000: 34). However, religious education was an important partner as the children would not understand the significance of some of the decisions Noor made without a knowledge and understanding of her beliefs and values.

This was a clear example of where cross-curricular planning and approaches work at their best. The children needed both historical and religious concepts, knowledge and understanding in order to benefit fully from a study of this little-known woman. We also agreed strongly with Barnes that 'the curriculum should be packed with opportunities for each child to find his or her strengths and activities which provide genuine challenge and multiple prospects for individual achievement' (Barnes, 2007: 6). By working in a variety of ways and in different environments we hoped to be able to introduce the pupils to more unusual activities which would stretch the more able but also provide the children with special needs a suitable level of challenge too. Our planning therefore followed these principles:

- Subjects included should arise from the topic.
- Lead with one subject, with cross-curricular activities arising from the central focus.
- Focus and drive the topic with key questions.
- Address the nature and the objectives of each subject included.
- Every topic will provide a context for literacy learning.

The head teacher was keen that the week also included some kind of 'wow' activity which would help to make the project more memorable. Due to the strong links between the university and Tullie House Museum, Carlisle, we were able to organize a sleepover for the children at the museum which would further broaden the range of activities and experiences that we were able to provide. This further strengthened the idea of involving a wide range of adults and audiences. The children were able to explore a range of Second World War artefacts and make identity cards and gas-mask boxes which they were required to carry everywhere. The air raid siren was set off several times over the evening to encourage the children to empathize with those who experienced this during the war. Following their discussions with older members of the community about air raids this made those experiences, which had been talked about, much more real and gave the evening impact, especially when we had evacuated to the bike shed outside and there was then an enormous roll of thunder! It may well be that the enduring memory of the week is related to this experience and not those back in the classroom. This is an important lesson for us in that we should be striving to include learning outside the classroom (DfES, 2006) at every opportunity to broaden the children's experiences and understanding of the world around them.

Links to key policy documents

Through this project we aimed to fulfil these aims taken from a variety of wider perspectives in addition to the National Curriculum itself. The QCA's *Big Picture* (2008) for example identifies that:

> The curriculum aims to enable all young people to become
>
> - Successful learners who enjoy learning, make progress and achieve
> - Confident individuals who are able to lead safe, healthy and fulfilling lives
> - Responsible citizens who make a positive contribution to society.

We considered new documentation, for example the *Every Child Matters: Change for Children* (DfES, 2004) agenda and the *Learning Outside the Classroom Manifesto* (DfES, 2006) as well as statutory expectations, in planning this project. We attempted to include a wide range of people, resources, different environments and events within this themed week, to match the needs and abilities of the children.

Challenging preconceptions

Children hold many preconceived ideas and stereotypes which are often not explored or addressed during their school life – sometimes staff may not even be aware of them. As the project developed we became aware that some children had different levels of understanding in some areas and we were able to address these issues. For example, several children thought that the religion of Islam had been followed in the past but that no one was a Muslim now. More obvious stereotypes were what princesses were capable of and that spies were men. Conversely, one or two children had very developed ideas which were not stereotypical at all. We deliberately explored these more general ideas in our first activity by asking the children to draw and annotate pictures of a princess and a spy. There were some interesting results – some very predictable – the spies were variously described as 'sinister', 'cool', 'sneaky', 'undercover', 'spooky' and 'disguisable'. More unusually they were also described as 'French', 'ugly', 'small', 'wear black clothing' and only one child had drawn the spy as a woman.

Child A also described her spy as 'half-sided'. When I asked her to elaborate on this she explained that 'you only get to know one side of a spy and you never know the other half'. Quite sophisticated reasoning for a 7-year-old! The images of both the spies and the princesses were obviously heavily influenced by the television programmes, stories and films the children had been exposed to. The princesses were portrayed as 'pretty', 'posh', 'happy', 'kind', 'special' and 'beautiful', but also 'distressed', 'proud', 'smart' and 'she is big because she ate too much'!

Developing the history component

(See WM 6.1.)

Knowledge skills and understanding (KSU) 1: Chronological understanding

The children were given a variety of photographs of Noor throughout her life. They were asked to order these chronologically. They worked in small groups and had to discuss and justify their decisions. An

Figure 6.2 Child's work: princess/spy

extension of this activity was undertaken by the Key Stage 2 children, which entailed producing their own time-lines of her life based on further research (also fulfils KSU 5).

KSU 2: Knowledge and understanding
All the activities helped to support this strand.

KSU 3: Historical interpretation
The children were introduced to Noor through a suitcase activity. The suitcase contained a sari, small paintbrushes, sheet music, a lipstick and necklace, a notebook and pen, a family photograph, an identity card and a magnifying glass.

The children were encouraged to consider each item and decide if the clues it provided gave them facts about the owner of the suitcase, or if they could make educated guesses about her. For example, the lipstick and necklace indicated that the owner was probably female and the ID card gave information about her, including her name, date of birth and height.

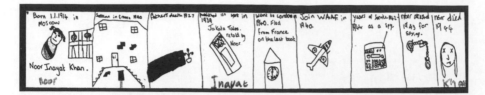

Figure 6.3　Time-line work

Three children working on timelines

After looking at phrases taken from the reports written about Noor during her training, they used them to write a reference for Noor, deciding for themselves which phrases they would include, as the phrases were both negative and positive.

The older members of the community were invited to talk about their memories of life during the Second World War. Prior to the oral history session the children prepared relevant questions to ask their visitors.

The children took part in a role-play activity where they assumed the roles of Noor, Buckmaster (Head of Special Operations Executive) and Vera Baker (Noor's immediate boss). Noor and Vera had to persuade Buckmaster that Noor was ready to be sent to Paris.

Child working on reports

KSU 4: Historical enquiry

The children used computers to access a variety of suitable websites to answer a set of given questions (available on the website WL 6.1–6.6). As an extension some children found extra dates related to Noor's life to add to their time-line.

The museum visit

Organizing a sleepover in the museum

This was one aspect of the week which worked extremely well – a testament to the staff at Tullie House who put in so much effort. There are many considerations as museums are usually under the control of the city or local council, so there may be slightly different regulations to abide by than those schools are used to. For example:

- The museum staff had to be confident that everyone had an up-to-date CRB check.
- Boys and girls had to sleep in separate areas of the museum – with implications for staffing.

- Separate toilet and washing facilities for each group may be necessary.
- An extra member of staff had to sleep in the room with all the alarms.
- Tullie House has a restaurant but arrangements for staff to work in the evening and early morning to make breakfasts had to be made.
- Arrangements for lighting, heating and any audio in the galleries had to be considered.
- Sleeping arrangements had to be arranged taking into account fire exits, and a fire drill had to be undertaken as part of the introductory talk.
- The local fire brigade and police should be informed if this is not a regular occurrence.
- Transport arrangements to and from the museum – parents brought the children to the museum on the Thursday evening and a bus returned them to school the next morning – staff therefore had to arrange lifts to the museum with their cars left at the school ready for the next day!
- Think carefully about which day to have the sleepover – you will not get much sleep so we would advise a Thursday evening so you only have to teach for one day before you can have a lie-in!

We were lucky that so many staff from the museum and school, and university students, were all prepared to give up their time for this, but there will be a minimum number of staff required for supervision. We all slept in sleeping bags but some of the children also had blow-up mattresses or yoga mats to make it a little more comfy. Some museums may not be big enough, or may not be prepared to allow you to sleep there. In this case, why not consider arranging the sleepover in the school itself?

As part of the museum visit, the children were involved in an artefacts activity. This was led by a museum education officer who was dressed in clothes from the time. The room had tables which were covered with a range of artefacts from this period in history. Volunteers were used to represent members of a family. As each child was chosen, information was given regarding their character. They were dressed in appropriate clothing and had to find artefacts that each character would have used. For example, Mr Bell caught rabbits to supplement the family's diet so the child was asked to find a suitable artefact that might have been used (a rabbit net). It caused great amusement that the toilet paper was just torn up newspaper!

KSU 5: Organization and communication

At the end of the week a whole-class assembly was held for the parents. The children decided themselves which information to present and in what order. The assembly included:

- the James Bond theme music played by three pupils on their guitars
- coded messages for the parents to decode for a prize
- rewritten stories from the Jakata Tales (children's stories written by Noor)

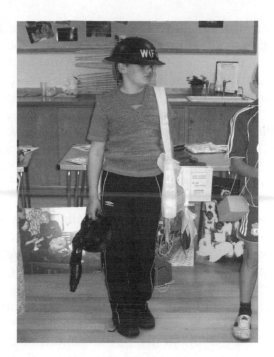

Child in period clothing

- examples of prayer mats and mendhi patterns
- time-lines and basic information about Noor's life
- songs from the time, for example, Run Rabbit Run.

Developing the religious education component

Learning about religion

> **The National Curriculum non-statutory guidance:**
>
> 1 Pupils should be taught to:
>
> (c) identify the importance, for some people, of belonging to a religion and recognize the difference this makes to their lives
>
> (d) explore how religious beliefs and ideas can be expressed through the arts and communicate their responses (from non-statutory national framework).

Activities to develop understanding of Islam
The following desirable learning outcomes were chosen:

- To know some of the basic facts about Islam.
- To understand what being a Muslim involves.
- To know and understand some of the symbols used in Islamic art.

The pupils were introduced to Noor's religion through a variety of activities. The children examined prayer beads and made prayer mats. The pattern and pictures point to the top of the mat as this will be facing Mecca. In Islamic art no animals or people can be represented. Muslims use plants, flowers and geometrical shapes. The patterns are usually symmetrical and use bright colours, for example red and gold. The Arabic alphabet and calligraphy using words to make patterns were also popular.

They learnt about the Qur'ān (Koran) and how precious it is to Muslims. This book is kept wrapped up and placed on the highest shelf in the room with nothing placed on top. Muslims must follow a special ritual of washing before reading this book. They also discussed that Muslims learn to read the Qur'ān which is written in another language (Arabic).

Further activities included talking to a teacher (Lisa MacGregor) who has experience of teaching Muslim children. The children were introduced to the different clothes that these children often wear out of school. As part of their school uniform these children have adapted versions, for example, wearing hijab (fitted headscarf) and khameez (long tunic) but in the school colours. The sari had been introduced during one of the history sessions. Many children were interested in the amount of time Muslim children spend at their mosques every day; this makes a significant difference to their lives. English is spoken as a second language for many of the Muslim children at Lisa's school. The children were encouraged to empathize with these children who have to learn through English, even though it is not their first language, and what this might feel like.

Learning from religion

> **The National Curriculum Non-statutory guidance:**
>
> 2. Pupils should be taught to:
>
> (e) recognize that religious teachings and ideas make a difference to individuals, families and the local community.

Lisa was able to explain how the fasting is accommodated in her school during the month of Ramadan. At the end of Ramadan the children celebrate Ĭd-ul-Fitr (*Eid*) which is a family time when everyone wears new clothes, exchanges cards and gifts, visits family and friends' houses and has a three-day feast of special foods. Women use henna to decorate their hands with elaborate patterns at this time and other special occasions. The children drew round their hands and designed their own mendhi patterns.

The children really grappled with the concept of fasting as this was something very new to most of them. Some children of their age actually attempt the fasting and the children tried hard to empathize with this idea.

The Great Corby children also struggled to come to terms with the fact that some Muslim children go to their mosque for two hours every night, leaving little time for the kinds of activities they normally did in the evenings.

The children were asked to think about how the sense of community is in some ways very similar to what they experience in their own small village. We tried to help the children understand that this religion helped Noor become strong and disciplined, which is why she could do what she did during the war.

Sufi, a branch of Islam

There are three main branches of Islam, one of which is Sufism. These Muslims use music, drumming and dance in their worship. Sufis are pacifists, this means they do not believe in violence and must always tell the truth. Muslims believe religion affects everything they do in their lives, so how they live their lives is very important to ensure they become close to God in paradise when they die. Sufis believe they can become close to God while alive. The term Sufi comes from the word *suf*, meaning wool. This is because Sufis wore clothes made of undyed wool as a way of demonstrating they had given up worldly goods and pleasures.

Once the children had grasped the basics of Islam they were then introduced to the idea that Noor was a Sufi pacifist Muslim. This was explained so the children could appreciate that there are different groups within Islam in the same way as Catholics, Methodists and Protestants are all Christians. This information had to be kept to quite a simple level but we wanted to ensure the children fully understood how Noor had been brought up to reject all forms of violence. These aspects were introduced through circle time discussions, with artefacts to engage and encourage questioning and discussion.

Developing the literacy component

Speaking and listening

Desirable learning outcomes:

To be able to listen and ask questions.
To be able to sustain listening and concentration while guests are speaking.

The whole week gave lots of opportunities for speaking and listening as so many extra adults were available for the children to talk to about and during the activities in the week. These ranged from university lecturers, visiting teachers, trainee teachers and older members of the local community, staff at the museum and family and friends. As previously mentioned, older members of the community were invited in to remember their Second World War childhoods. Some of these people were rather hard of hearing so the children had to take this into account when asking their questions. The children were also encouraged to try and stay on the topic and take into account previous questions and answers during discussions. In some instances the reminiscences varied considerably; this helped the children to appreciate different experiences of the war.

The children took part in a role-play activity in small groups and a whole-school assembly (see history activities, WM 6.2 web material) which developed their language skills further.

Reading

Desirable learning outcomes:

To be able to extract information from a variety of texts.
To be able to use the organizational features of websites to find information.

In order to find out about Noor and her life, the children accessed a range of appropriate websites. They had to navigate their way through these sites to find relevant information, which was used to inform their writing. The children also had to read some simple primary sources. These were carefully chosen to ensure appropriate reading levels.

Writing

Desirable learning outcomes:

To be able to write full sentences with correct punctuation.
To understand that writing differs depending on purpose and audience.
To be able to order events and include detail.

A variety of written tasks was undertaken by the children. These included writing letters and diary entries in role as Noor, writing a reference for Noor as well as making notes from the websites to aid their writing. A time-line of Noor's life was also devised. For the whole-school assembly the children wrote individual invitations to their family and friends giving relevant information.

Developing numeracy

> ### *Desirable learning outcomes:*
>
> To be able to use number to solve problems.
> To be able to use mental strategies to solve problems.
> To know basic number facts up to ten.
> To be able to use and write coordinates.

These activities were approached with the premise that this was the kind of training spies would have received. Spies need to be able to follow instructions, solve codes and read clues. The children were encouraged to undertake the activities in 'role' as spies with the teacher acting as the head of MI5. On a carousel of activities, making use of the extra available adults, the pupils were given two maps with differing scales and they had to find the coordinates of particular significant landmarks in the village and in the playground. They then had to follow a set of instructions around the playground finding letter clues to unscramble in order to identify a word (superspy!). Obviously this activity had strong links with geography as well as numeracy. A further task was to follow instructions to programme the Beebots (a programmable electronic toy). On another day the children had to work out basic number facts, differentiated to their ability, in order to work out a code name for themselves. They were all given a code-breaker and they then had to work out their own set of clues. The children had been allocated names, depending on their own particular interests and hobbies.

They then had to work as a group to work out further clues, find the double agent and break the clue of where the treasure was hidden. It was interesting that the children did not view either of these lessons as numeracy as one child asked on the third morning, 'Are we not doing any numeracy this week?' The children thoroughly enjoyed these activities and some were obviously not aware just how much they were practising their numeracy skills.

Values

We wanted the children to begin to appreciate why Noor made some of the decisions she did, which were influenced by her beliefs.

Much of this information was introduced to the children gradually over the week. We did not go into details about her death in the concentration camp as we felt this was unnecessary with children of this age. Many of the children were able to grasp why she had left her weapon

'Though she firmly believed that Britain should give Indians their freedom, Noor was convinced that Indian leaders should not press for independence when Britain had its hands full fighting the war. She felt that if the Indians backed Britain and won many gallantry medals it would create a sense of confidence in them, and the British would readily grant independence to India after the war' (Basu, 2006: 45).

Noor left Paris and fled to England where she decided to support the allies against the Nazis as she felt they were the greater threat to personal liberty and she believed that by making her own small contribution this would help to work towards the greater aim of Indian independence. She joined the WAAF in order to do this in a non-violent way, as she was a pacifist (non-violent). Originally she trained as a wireless operator. This was very different from the life she was used to but Noor was determined to adapt to it. Following her training she worked transmitting and receiving messages. Although this was allowing her to work in a non-violent job helping the cause, she still had to make many compromises in her day-to-day life as she was not openly living as a Sufi Muslim. Noor hid all personal details about her previous life from her new colleagues, even to the point of adopting a more British name (Nora Baker) and appearing to follow the Church of England faith. Once Noor was identified as a possible Special Operations Executive (SOE) officer, or spy, the expectation that she might have to use violent actions became more apparent. She was trained to use firearms, though her superiors commented she appeared to be frightened of these weapons. Although she went through the training she actually left her gun behind when she was sent to Paris.

Figure 6.4   Further information about Noor Inayat Khan

behind and explain and give explanations for this. One child explained 'because of her being a Muslim she wasn't allowed to kill people' and another clarified 'she wouldn't want to take it in case she used it in a bad situation because she wouldn't be able to forgive herself'. It is clear from comments like this the children were able to begin to give explanations for Noor's motives.

In order to fully understand Noor and her values, the children needed to learn about Noor's life and her beliefs together, not as two different aspects of the curriculum, but as two strands of one woman's life. Although this project was limited to a week we felt the children had begun to understand why Noor had made the decision to become a spy. By this point they had learned a great deal about her life and religion, and we wanted to see to what extent they were beginning to grasp the values she held dear. At the sleepover we were able to talk to the children informally about their feelings about the activities and Noor herself and gauge their understanding of the dilemmas she faced. We were impressed by the discussions the children could hold, making their points and backing these up with quite sophisticated reasoning.

It is often through the content that it is easiest to combine subjects but we do need to be careful to ensure that the integrity of the subject itself is not lost. The children needed to learn not only about Noor and her life, but also to develop some of the skills of being a historian; asking relevant questions, enquiry, deducting, classifying, interpreting, comparing, organizing and communicating what they have discovered – all important historical skills. The choice of Noor Inayat Khan as the focus of the project seemed to work extremely well. As the staff were intrigued by Noor, their enthusiasm was communicated to the children who became equally interested in this woman's unusual life. There had been some concerns expressed that perhaps we were expecting too much of the younger children, but this proved to be unfounded and in fact the children exceeded our expectations. This is another important lesson – do not underestimate the abilities of your children, and of younger pupils in particular.

Conclusions

The overwhelming feeling of all those involved in this project was that, although it was a great deal of work, it was ultimately extremely successful. Comments included:

- 'Lots of work but worth it.'
- 'You won't fit it all in but go with the flow.'
- 'It was fun for teachers and pupils.'
- 'The children (and us!) learnt a lot.'
- 'Do it – it's worthwhile – it's a lot of work but good teamwork helps with this.'

Overall the staff felt the week worked very well for the children too. The teachers commented 'the children learnt a lot', 'enjoyed the interaction with other adults', and 'they had learnt loads by the end of the week, they didn't see it as lessons; seemed as though the pressure was off and so they learnt and remembered much more'. Evidently it was felt the children had gained a great deal from this way of working. Barnes (2007: 9) commented that children learn best 'in cross curricular and authentic contexts' and it was a hope that this context would prove to be authentic for everyone involved. This was particularly relevant in the literacy and numeracy activities, as they gave the children a concrete context in which to practise their skills. The teachers felt this was particularly important as so often these subjects are taught in isolation without this context. With the push to improve standards, we must not forget that children need to develop and practise their skills in a variety of situations in order to internalize these abilities.

The staff felt that with some help and support they would be able and more than willing to attempt this kind of project again. Teachers commented that they would need 'the support of an appropriate professional' and 'links with the students, Tullie House etc., which are essential', while another felt 'a pack to guide you' would be useful. I think the staff are underestimating their own knowledge and capabilities here. I can see that help in identifying suitable themes or projects would be useful but I am sure the vast majority of teachers, especially working as a team within their own schools, could organize a project just as successful as this one proved to be.

References

Barnes, J. (2007) *Cross-Curricular Learning 3–14*. London: Paul Chapman Publishing.

Basu, S. (2006) *Spy Princess: The Life of Noor Inayat Khan*. London: Sutton Publishing.

Claire, H. (1996) *Reclaiming Our Pasts – Equality and Diversity in the Primary History Curriculum*. London: Trentham Books.

Cooper, H. (2000) *The Teaching of History in Primary Schools*. 3rd edn. London: David Fulton.

Department for Education and Skills (DfES) (2004) *Every Child Matters: Change for Children*. London: DfES Publications.

Department for Education and Skills (DfES) (2006) *Learning Outside the Classroom Manifesto*. London: DfES Publications.

Qualification and Curriculam Authority (QCA) (2008) *The Big Picture*. Draft. London: DfES Publications. Available at www.qca.org.uk/libraryAssets/images/big-picture-curriculum. (Accessed 1 December 2008.)

Also used 'Liberte: The Life of Noor Inayat Khan' written by Year 6 children, Chorlton Charch of England Primary School, Manchester, available from Ahmed Iqbal Ullah Race Relations Resource Centre, Ground Floor, Devonshire House, University Precinct Centre, Oxford Road, Manchester, M13 9PL.

Weblinks (see also the website of this book)
The websites we found were aimed mainly at adults so have to be used with care:

WL6.1 www.bbc.co.uk/history/historic_figures/inayat_khan_noor.shtml

WL6.2 www.historylearningsite.co.uk/noor_inayat_khan.htm

WL6.3 www.writespirit.net/authors/noor_inayat_khan

WL6.4 www.spartacus.schoolnet.co.uk/SOEnoor.htm

WL6.5 www.bbc.co.uk/history/programmes/timewatch/gallery_spy_06.shtml

WL6.6 www.the-south-asian.com/Sept2001/Noor%20Inayat%20Khan1.htm

7

Comparing life today with someone's in the past: history, geography, literacy, mathematics, science, art, design and technology

Jen Ager

Chapter introduction

This chapter needs to be read in conjunction with the Teachers TV programme that accompanies it (WL 7.1) and associated analysis video and resources on the same site. Here Jen Ager describes the challenges and the rewards of planning and teaching an intensive week looking at the values of Tudor explorers and leads on to the key themes identified in the Teachers TV analysis video: identifying the values specific to the time; historical thinking; questioning; progression and finally shared enquiry. The history-focused project draws on a number of other areas of the curriculum.

Tudor exploration and settlement

Rationale for a cross-curricular approach

The Department for Education and Skills (DfES) stresses that schools have freedom to teach in a cross-curricular way:

> Within the curriculum, teachers and schools have the freedom to decide how to arrange learning in school today – there is no requirement for subjects to be taught discretely – they can be grouped or taught through subjects – if strong enough links are created between subjects, pupils' knowledge and skills can be used across the whole curriculum. (DfES, 2003: 17)

It was apparent, when I started planning this topic, that it could provide a fantastic opportunity for cross-curricular planning and, on closer
inspection, through considering values and attitudes of people in the
past, many aspects of personal, social and health education permeated
the topic; for example, developing empathy for others, tolerance, fairness and justice, challenging stereotypes. The values underpinning
each objective are highlighted in the medium-term plan (WM 7.1).
'Interdisciplinary/cross-curricular teaching involves a conscious effort
to apply knowledge, principles, and/or values to more than one academic discipline simultaneously. The disciplines may be related
through a central theme, issue, problem, process, topic or experience'
(Jacobs, 1989: 54).

The planning process

When I first began to consider my plans for investigating the question,
'Why did the Tudors explore outside Europe?', I asked myself what exactly
I wanted the children to achieve from the unit. I did some research and
scribbled my ideas under headings. By involving other subjects in this
enquiry, children at different levels of maturity and ability and with different learning styles could engage with it through a variety of different
practical and enjoyable activities.

I jotted down my headings and notes:

- Why?
  Explorers: competition with Spain/national pride – money, (piracy), plunder,
  trade, new trade routes.
  Settlers: over-population, new ways of life, own religious practices and beliefs.
- How?
  Life on board ship, galleons, working children, diet, new navigation equipment.
- Impact on our lives today.
  Changes in geographical understanding – earth not flat, world maps, charts
  for sailors, scientific discoveries – navigational aids, trade – London trading
  companies, beginnings of globalization, new diseases, new foods.

As a result I found a plethora of questions building up in my
mind. How was I to teach all this in a block of seven history lessons? What were the cross-curricular opportunities under each
heading? What were the opportunities to build in values education? How could I tackle some of the more complicated issues in
such a short period of time? What conceptual understanding did I
want the children to reach?

As a result of the wealth of subject matter available it was decided to
teach this unit in a targeted focus week. One advantage of this was that

the children would find it easier to concentrate their thinking. It is interesting to contrast this with the long-term theme used in Chapter 8 where a different type of theme benefited from the opportunity to return to ideas as they developed. Here, however, it was clear that a strong focus would benefit from the intensive model.

Nevertheless, as a result of the nature of my class, I decided to keep numeracy sessions mainly separate and in the mornings, enabling the keen mathematicians in the group to maintain the impetus of the current work in numeracy.

Activities planned in different subjects, which have a values dimension, and are central to the enquiry

The planning process involved particular challenges because of the decision to integrate a values dimension. I needed to devise activities which would enable children to consider the points of view, behaviour and motivations of people in the past, and to express their own opinions about them. I was aware of the controversial and often emotional aspects of history, particularly when studying what we would now see as unfair treatment of others, and that this may also be the case where there are disparities between what is taught in school history, family/community histories and other histories (WL 7.2). We have to be careful about discussing religious differences, treatment of indigenous peoples, population growth, emigration, and so on.

Figure 7.1 shows how I planned to combine different subjects within the enquiry, 'Why did the Tudors explore outside Europe?' WM 7.1 shows the medium-term plan for these activities. WM 7.2 is the timetable of the cross-curricular theme over one week.

History

I had decided that the content of the enquiry would be why and how the Tudors undertook journeys of exploration and their impact on our world today. These big questions would be explored as open-ended questions through discussion, in relation to different practical activities.

I made a mental note to remember that discussion, in history, is concerned with questions of time and change, causes and effects, or with discussing what artefacts are, how they may have been made and used by people in the past, and, most importantly, that sometimes there is no right answer – although opinions must be supported with reasons. The activities I decided upon are listed below.

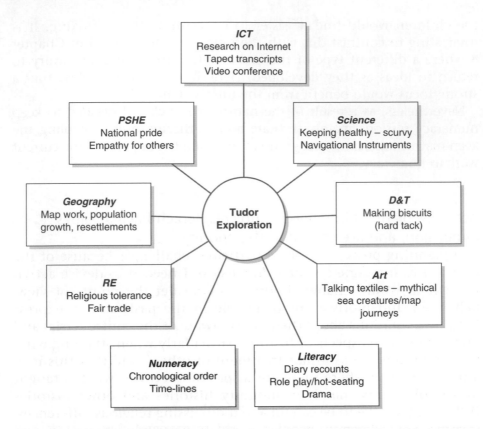

Figure 7.1 A model of how the theme could be taught simultaneously in other subject areas

History activities

1 Theatre workshop. Before the week of the project, the children embarked on an intensive day working with the Lynx Theatre Workshop (Lynx Theatre in Education Project) to produce a 'Play in a Day' on the subject of Tudor explorers, which would be performed to the rest of the school. The aim was to nurture their imagination and creative thinking. It was to be a shared experience which enabled everyone to access some of the more complex history content I planned to cover.

2 Concept maps. The first activity of the week was to make concept maps showing what the children already knew about Tudor explorers, using symbols, words and pictures. Everyone felt able to attempt this, following the play-making session.

3 Time-lines and maps. Large time-lines and maps, showing different journeys of exploration and of settlement in Roanoke, were made for the classroom walls, using secondary sources, reference books and the Internet. These could be used for future reference.

(Weblink 7.3.)

Sketching and planning a journey

Figure 7.2   An example of a concept map

History and information and communication technology

I wanted to make learning as interactive and enjoyable as possible but, in rural Cumbria, we did not have immediate access to any museums on seafaring and were not within easy reach of a coastline to stimulate or excite children. After further Internet research I found that I could book an interactive lesson on Tudor explorers with an expert at the National Maritime Museum in Greenwich. This worked extremely well. At 10.00, dead on cue, we were connected with the museum. Throughout, the children were able to talk to the museum educator, ask questions and see exhibits. It was truly interactive and connected us with an expert in a world famous museum who could help us with our enquiries. I thoroughly recommend it.

The film crew

While teaching this week we had Teachers TV filming for two days in order to make two programmes based on exploring Tudor values. This added another dimension to the week and the class learnt a lot of media and film techniques, alongside performing in front of an audience.

Activities involving history, literacy and empathy

A huge amount of speaking and listening skills were involved as many lessons were discussion based and involved small groups

History, explorers, literacy and understanding others

1 Poetry. In one session the children lined up outside the classroom door in silence after break, in order to walk through a 'magic arch' made by two children in the doorway. This enabled them to enter a totally blacked-out room except for a candle on each table. There was a hush of expectation as I moved around the tables with my candle, reading (*The Golden Hind*, Rona Dixon, February 2006; WL 7.4). This describes the life of a cabin boy on a sailing ship, the weather, the dark and cramped conditions, fear and loneliness. Any immediate follow-up was unnecessary and would have ruined the powerful effect.

2 Hot-seating. Attempts to bring the whole experience to life included using hot-seating and role-play situations to make historical figures 'come alive' in the children's eyes. (On the video there is a wonderful clip of the children generating questions to put to Sir Francis Drake.) The children first generated and wrote down their questions, when Sir Francis (identified by the pewter jug he carried as a stimulus and prop) emerged. 'He' was able to give valid answers to their questions using knowledge from previous lessons.

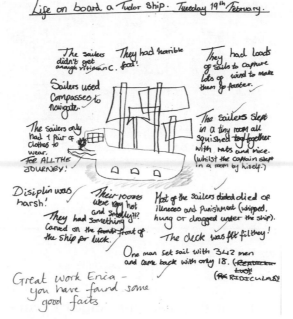

Figure 7.3   Life on board a Tudor ship

Later children wrote more questions for 'an ordinary sailor' who was able to give them a very different picture of life on board, much of it drawn from the poem the children had heard and from a discussion of weevils, rats, scurvy and 'hard tack'.

History, literacy and settlers, and understanding others

A visit to the wild shores of Virginia: emotional literacy, tolerance, indigenous peoples and fairness.

After finding out about explorers we considered Tudor people who chose to emigrate and settle in Roanoke in America, which was renamed Virginia. (As Rosa said, 'The people who lived there might have been a little bit cross because they'd given it their own name and they come along and rename it'.)

Children discussed why they might have decided to come here and questions of religious tolerance, the initial generosity of the Native Americans, the possible reasons why their feelings changed, including exploitation by the settlers, and the mysterious reasons for the settlers' disappearance.

But to engage children's imagination, before I embarked on these quite complex discussions, we first made our way, on a very cold, rainy and windy afternoon, down the farm path opposite the school until all we could see were hills, grass and trees, with no sign of habitation. The

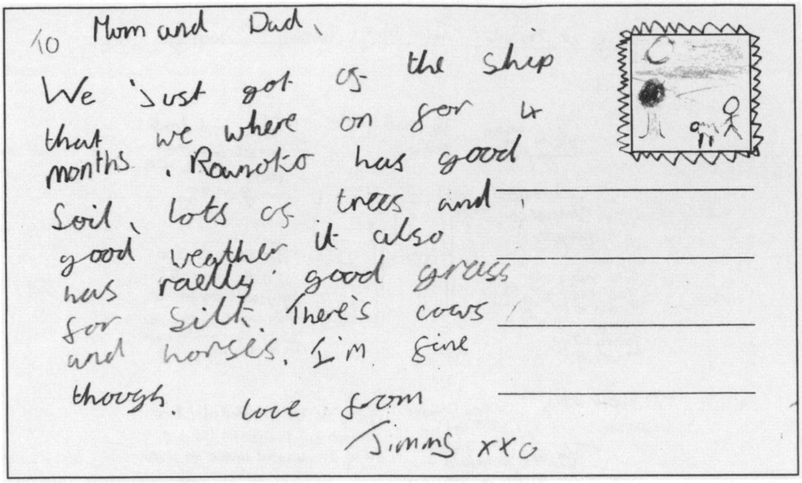

To Mom and Dad,
We just got of the ship that we where on for 4 months. Ranoko has good soil, lots of trees and good weather it also has raelly good grass for silt. There's cows and horses. I'm fine though. Love from Jimms xxo

Figure 7.4 A message from Roanaoke

children were told that they had just landed in America. They discussed what they would need to do to provide themselves with shelter, warmth and food in the immediate and longer term, using only the resources they could see or knew could be found here.

Back in the warm classroom they worked in groups to sequence activities on cards in order to prioritize what they must do to survive. This gave rise to some interesting differences of opinion; for example would it be a good idea to start trying to convert the indigenous people, and if not, why not?

I persuaded my reluctant husband to record a first-hand account of what life was like in Roanoke written by one of the settlers (WL 7.5). Children used atlases to follow the journey. Then they discussed knowledge they had about life on board ship from the poetry, the vast distances and time involved, and awareness of how they and other people might be feeling. Children were asked to imagine that they were part of this party of settlers and write their own message home, describing their feelings and experiences and how life had changed since they had left England. Figure 7.4 shows one of their messages.

History, art and design

Drawing artefacts
These were borrowed from Tullie House Museum, Carlisle (for example, leather plate, pewter jug, boatswain's whistle, astrolabe). Children then wrote descriptive captions saying what they thought they were, how

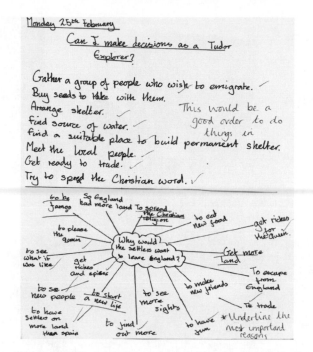

Figure 7.5 A pupil tries to understand why anyone would emigrate in Tudor times

they were made and who may have used them. These were used later in a hot-seating activity.

I used the QCA document *Talking Textiles* (QCA, 2000) to plan another art activity. In response to accounts and poems from sailors, symbols used in maps in the Tudor period and from their own imagination, children sketched mythical sea creatures. They used these sketches to design and make their own mythical sea creature. The individual pieces were then joined together as an account of Tudor sailors' response to and feelings about the sea.

History, science, design and technology and understanding others

Hard tack

I consulted the National Curriculum objective 5a, 'Keeping healthy', and decided that making 'hard tack' would be an interesting way to get children of all abilities to think about diet, food conservation and health, and to understand a little better the hardships of Tudor explorers. They made it, in small groups, and ate it the following day with water and salted meat.

Using flour, salt and water to make hard tack – a seafarer's standard fare

Teacher: What is hard tack made of?
Pupil: Water, salt and flour.
Teacher: Is it tasty? Think, when all the fresh food ran out this could have been
            one of the few things they would have on board to eat.
Pupil: It must have been horrible. It would have rats on and weevils. They'd get
            scurvy. That's what the lady at the Maritime Museum was talking about.
Teacher: What's scurvy?
Pupil: It's when your gums bleed, your teeth fall out and you haven't eaten
            enough vitamins.

History and geography

Children studied maps, globes and measurement of distance and time, discussed population growth in Tudor times and today and its implications, where to create a new settlement and how this might be done using available resources, and the effects of weather. However there were no discrete geography lessons.

Mathematics

Again there were no discrete lessons in mathematics but there was much use of time-lines at the beginning of the topic and measurement of time and distance using ratio and scale. My main aim was not to expect the children to remember precise dates but to have some understanding of where the Tudors stand in relation to other periods they have learned about, how long ago this was and the times and distances involved in the voyages.

What others said about the project

Martha in class 5: 'I like doing different things mixed up with the Tudors, like Tudors mixed in with literacy. It's cool because you do history in all different types of things. You learn loads.'

Two viewers of the television programmes: 'Fantastic work by this teacher! Really useful learning experiences and an inspiration to my own teaching of this subject through the curriculam areas' and 'We are just starting to introduce cross-curricular topic work in our school next academic year. Great idea to take a whole week to really immerse the children in the topic. I loved the way the children were taught historical thinking and to ask open questions. I'm sure this class will remember that week well into their adulthood. Great stuff.'

Such comments made the trauma of being televised for a week worthwhile!

References

Department for Education and Skills (DfES) (2003) *Excellence and Enjoyment: A Strategy for Primary Schools*. London: DfES.

Jacobs, H. (1989) *Interdisciplinary Curriculum: Design and Implementation*. Alexandria, VA: Association for Supervision and Curriculam Development.

Lynx theatre in education project. Tel: 0161 6780804.

Qualifications and Curriculum Authority (QCA) (2000) *Talking Textiles*. Art & Design KS1 and KS2 Unit 5C Talking Textiles. London: QCA.

Thinking through environmental values: planning for a long-term cross-curricular theme using local change and partnership – geography, art and science

Chris Rowley

Chapter introduction

Here Chris Rowley of the University of Cumbria works with Cheryl Johnston of Goodly Dale School, Belinda Fear of Elleray Preparatory School and Kelley Sproston of The National Trust, St Catherine's, Windermere. The chapter investigates the impact of a two-year project in which children are involved in planning and using a new 'eco-friendly' learning building created for The National Trust's 'Footprint Project'. It emerges that the children moved through a series of changes in their vision of both the building and the environment during the project, benefiting particularly from the long-term nature of the partnership and the cross-curricular nature of the work. The length of the project enabled children to move through temporary confusion into greater understanding of some key concepts in environmental education.

This chapter, together with the case study that it describes, starts from the now widespread belief that changing how we think must be central to any serious attempt at education for a rapidly changing environment. (Bonnett, 2004; Orr, 2004; Sterling and Schumacher

Society, 2001) Ever since *Homo sapiens* emerged as a dominant species a key to that dominance has been the ability to think into the future, to see consequences and thereby change our actions in order to manage the future to our own advantage. That remarkable ability to think both reflectively and proactively for our benefit may be one of the key factors that has led to the problems of resource depletion, climate change and mass extinction that surrounds us. Of course, education does not in any way bear full responsibility for this, particularly given the very recent emergence of mass formalized education in the history of our species. It is, indeed, self-evident that education cannot, alone, provide the solution either. There is, however, no doubt that how we educate the next generation can play a very substantial role in nudging our culture in new directions. The big question is, can we use the same thinking to solve these problems?

The case study in this chapter offers an example of long-term, cross-curricular planning which draws together some of the very best approaches to teaching and learning. It uses approaches which draw upon a stunning stimulus to move children, through creative teaching, clear strategies to develop rigorous thinking and opportunities for the inclusion of children with a variety of abilities and learning styles, culminating in positive action and reflective evaluation. In many ways the project described led to a shift in thinking which goes some way towards meeting the challenges identified above.

At its heart is the notion of developing children's values regarding the environment through a long-term, cross-curricular theme delivered in partnership with a local group (in this case The National Trust) involved in innovative change.

It is rare for a teacher to be able to achieve so much, yet here that is exactly what happened, the result of a range of factors, partly planned, partly coincidental, partly inspirational, but nevertheless possible as a result of a range of cross-curricular opportunities which involved:

- a deliberately long-term (18 months) theme.
- an effective partnership (in this case with The National Trust and an artist, Jac Scott)
- opportunities for redirection through flexible planning (see WM 8.1 for an art medium-term plan which linked well into the visits)
- specific cross-curricular pedagogies bringing together artistic and practical alongside philosophical and scientific (these are discussed in this chapter)
- opportunities for children to contribute to the direction of the theme, and in some instances the objective as well
- recognition of the importance of children being given the motivation of passing their findings on to others, both in the school and at home

When we began the footprint project in Year 4 I knew very little about the environment, global warming and climate change. Since we have been taught by Gareth, Jac and Kelley that has all changed. I know how important it is to reuse and recycle. I have now learnt why it is good to buy food locally and not to drive everywhere, take less baths and more showers and finally use more public transport, cycle more or just walk. When I'm older and have a house of my own I will try to save as much energy as I do now.
(Hannah Santamera, Windermere C.E. Junior School)

Figure 8.1   A child's evaluation of the Footprint Project

Recycling sign (photograph: Jac Scott)

- audits of individual and whole-school impact developing personal as well as group responsibility
- regular visits to a changing place over a period of 18 months, with clear efforts to link that place to the children's own school and experiences
- outdoor experiences offering chances for children to ask questions which just are not asked indoors.

Put together over a long period these elements of the case study led to clear indications of lifestyle changes amongst significant numbers of the children who took part. The purpose of this chapter is to attempt to unpick why and how this approach was successful.

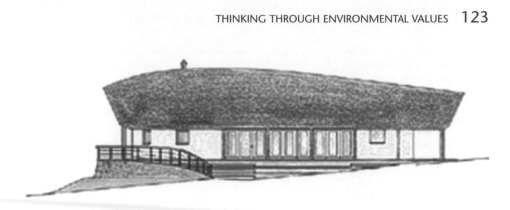

The footprint building design sketch (image: The National Trust)

The case study

The case study used in this chapter involved four schools in the South Lakes area of Cumbria (Elleray Preparatory, Windermere Juniors, Staveley, Goodly Dale), in a partnership with The National Trust at St Catherine's, Troutbeck Bridge, over a period of 18 months from June 2006 to November 2007. The focus for the partnership was the building of a learning base at The National Trust St Catherine's estate, known as the 'Footprint Project'. This building was designed to raise questions concerning the materials that we use, how we use them and where they

Nest made of lime and wood (photograph: Jac Scott)

Participants will learn:
That we all have an impact on the world through our actions.
That the choices we make in our lives can make a difference to the environment, locally and globally.
That to reduce the size of our ecological footprint is a good thing.
To name at least two things they can do to help reduce their footprint size.
That the new building at St Catherine's is an example of an environmentally friendly building.
Creative and artistic techniques in the medium that they work in.
They will understand how the final piece relates to the footprint theme.
Behavioural Objectives
Participants will want to:
Take at least one personal action, that they can realistically do, that reduces their footprint size.
Suggest three things, as a class, which their school could adopt to reduce the footprint size and to develop a plan that enables these suggestions to be implemented.
Lead an assembly in their school about the project that explains not only the project but also some of the issues behind it.
Participants will:
Feel that it is important for people to minimise our resource use.
Care that a large ecological footprint is bad for the environment.
Feel that they can positively address these issues through their own actions and to feel that this is a valid and important contribution.

Figure 8.2   Footprint Project initial objectives

come from. The use of car tyres, straw bales, limewash, local wood, sheep's wool and other local resources made this an ideal opportunity to involve children from local primary schools with The National Trust.

The project was founded on a series of objectives which carefully integrated aspects of values education alongside a clear development of conceptual knowledge. To do this, conceptual understanding took precedence over subject understanding, since many of the concepts involved in understanding the building required an appreciation of different areas of the curriculum. Understanding the links between the building's shape (see Figure 8.2) and its function, for example, can only be appreciated with some understanding of the science, geography and artistic elements of the design. A cross-curricular approach is the only approach appropriate to a project like this.

Initial objectives of the project

This case study focuses on children of class 4/5/6 at Goodly Dale School with their teacher, Cheryl Johnston, and children of Years 5 and 6 from Ellerey School, Windermere, with their Year 6 teacher Belinda Fear. It involved two phases over 18 months shown in the Figure 8.3.

Those involved were consistent in recognizing the importance of the long-term nature of this project in enabling it to achieve its outcomes.

Phase 1 March–June 06	Introduction in schools to new terms and concepts, with a baseline assessment of what they understand by 'sustainable' & 'climate change'. Discussions of how our behaviour impacts on the environment and what we can do to reduce that in the future. Sound recordings were made of the children and evaluation material collected.
June–July 06	Initial visit by children to the site & orientation. Introduction to project and construction of building, outline of materials used. Session in woods looking at natural shelters, comparing features such as location, design, materials and how it fits the purpose.
September–October 06	Footprint and in school sessions focused on a quiz to guide Internet research on the lifecycle of materials (timber, wool, straw and lime, clay and rubber), which they displayed in a poster to share with others. Went on to look at impacts of manufacturing materials and links between processes, the energy required and what effect CO_2 has on climate change. Why and how using these materials were going to help.
November–December 06	(NT) Community Learning Officer and Jac Scott, artist, in school to draw research together and present in an engaging art form. Worked with their materials to create giant nests with straw and lime and miniature bales of straw and clay to echo wall construction materials and methods.
May 07	Art Installations displayed at Footprint in Opening Ceremony – all 145 children plus teachers attended.
June–July 07	NT worked with Lake District National Park Authority to help children focus on auditing their own resource use in school – Goodly Dale decided to focus on recycling, energy and water use. Presented their findings and action plans in class and whole school assemblies. Completed the 'Footprint Calculator' activity to come up with a score for their own personal Footprint – lead into thinking about how they could individually change their behaviour to bring their own Footprint Score down. They drew around their feet on reused card and wrote pledges for how they would try to waste fewer resources over their summer holidays.
Phase 2 September–October 07	We took each school on a high impact trip to give a wider perspective to the issues and topics they were thinking about. Goodly Dale went to see the Cockermouth EcoCentre, a Renewable Energy Project. We then held in school artist workshops to plan for the next art installation project – 'Body Mapping & Signage'. Worked in small groups on massive ideas sheets to come up with signage designs, messages and locations. The NT CLO and Jac then facilitated four hands-on sessions per school using waste and recycled materials to create life, size, innovative signage based on the children themselves, each one focusing on either water, energy use or paper and waste to get important messages across to the rest of the school and the wider community and help raise awareness and reduce their environmental footprint.
November 07	Each school then prepared 'Final Performances' at assemblies to showcase their work and share their ideas with fellow pupils, other staff at the school and parents to help them understand the impact of their school's energy and resource waste on the environment and to help them transfer their ideas to home.

Figure 8.3 The development of this long-term project in partnership with The National Trust

The Headteacher of Staveley Primary School, Mike Prince, found that learning had become embedded (in that children applied their learning across the curriculum). He also commented on the importance of the long-term link to an individual outside the school, someone who the children identified with the project. Similar observations were made by Belinda Fear, the teacher at Elleray, where the Footprint Project was seen as a 'springboard' for other learning. Cheryl Johnston of Goodly Dale noted that children's behaviour changed both out of school and in it, largely because of the long timescale of the project's development.

Figure 8.4   Embedded learning

This consistency has led to a focus for this chapter in considering some of the implications of such long-term projects for planning, teaching and learning a cross-curricular theme.

Long-term partnership planning

The key ingredients of such a partnership involve developing under-standing of change over time; that change could be for good or bad, and should be a change that raises questions. In terms of good environmental education this approach makes it possible to drive a long-term project from a local issue. It avoids starting from big abstract concepts such as climate change, which so often plague environmental education and are often difficult to relate to real action.

There seems to be evidence that a cross-curricular project like this offers an 'added extra' of enhanced learning in other curriculum areas. The essence of this long-term (18 months) project could equally be found in a variety of other contexts:

- a new housing development and partnership with a local building company
- new energy provision in an area (a wind turbine?) and partnership with a local energy supplier
- a local recycling project

This approach is by no means new. There were once numerous examples of good practice built upon long-term observation of change, such as Palmer and Wise (1982). Indeed, the QCA offers examples of long-term schemes to promote this type of cross-curricular planning in schools. These are called 'continuous units'. An example is unit 18 in geography, 'Connecting ourselves to the world'. The generally low take-up of these long-term schemes may be a result of the significant changes in the expectations of teachers and schools that have taken place in intervening years, which have made the process of planning for long-term themes more difficult. The lack of take-up may also reflect the lack of a clear and recognizable context in many of these schemes. Planning has rightly been given a pivotal role in the teaching process, but it is clear from this long-term partnership project that the nature of planning needs to be very different from the models that we use for short-and medium-term themes. The QCA, through its futures programme, is clearly now encouraging schools to find new ways of connecting subjects, skills and values, and yet long-term themes are rarely seen. Development of values through cross-curricular teaching and learning over longer periods needs to be reactive to context as it develops. But also it needs, perhaps, a different way of seeing the curriculum, one where context is important but also where particular concepts are developed slowly and in greater depth. These concepts need themselves to be open to questioning and controversy if children are to have genuine opportunities for real enquiry. In this project the concept of materials was, for example, developed gradually. This enabled children to consider the influence of our values on the choice of which materials would be most suited to the building.

A particularly interesting paper by John Hattie (2003) attempted to create a synthesis of over 500,000 studies of effects on student achievement, and in so doing identified those features that have a greater than average effect on learning. Hattie was able to identify characteristics of what he called 'expert teaching', and in doing so recognized a number of key factors which go to make what he calls an 'expert' as distinct from an 'experienced' teacher. Two of his findings have particular significance in the long-term cross-curricular and value-laden work involved in this case study.

'Expert' teachers are more context-dependent. They recognize, for example, how their planning might be influenced by the place. The circumstances of specific days and the setting available for learning. Children at Goodly Dale recognized that the school already did recycling so they chose to focus on water and electricity use. In doing this they were able to steer the enquiry into their own context. Children's involvement is fundamental to this. The development of the project opened up opportunities which could not have been foreseen. As such, children benefited from being involved to some extent in the direction of the work, particularly in phase 2. In addition, the teacher was able to capitalize on opportunities that arose in the broader curriculum.

'Expert' teachers also, according to Hattie, have deeper representations about teaching and learning. 'Experts' and 'experienced' teachers do not differ in the amount of knowledge that they have, but in how they organize and use this knowledge. Experts possess knowledge that is more integrated, in that they combine subject matter with content knowledge, and can relate current lesson content to other subjects in the curriculum, changing and adding to them according to their students' needs and their own goals. (Hattie, 2003: 6–7) It seems here that Hattie

'… because we gave the children so much freedom in both phases to work together in small teams to make decisions, plan and audit their resource use, design and create art installations and perform presentations, they have really taken an ownership of the development and outcomes of this project and obviously felt empowerment to make a difference themselves.' (Kelley Sproston, National Trust)

'… Children began to take responsibility both for themselves and for their families in the promotion of different environmental behaviours.' (Cheryl Johnston, Teacher, Goodley Dale School)

Figure 8.5   Taking ownership

is identifying conceptual knowledge as enabling expert teachers to make connections between different types of knowledge.

It seems that this was illustrated through this case study in a number of ways, and has some implications for planning work of this kind. Emerging concepts are central. The individual subjects in this study were able to demonstrate greater levels of rigour because of the concepts that emerged. Because the initial objectives were based around a number of big concepts, opportunities arose at a number of stages to elaborate aspects of these. An example from this project would be the concept of choice, which was embedded in the original objectives of the project and was developed in different circumstances and different contexts:

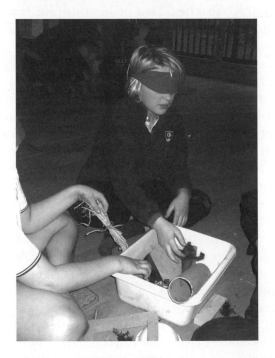

Choosing the 'best material' (photograph: Belinda Fear)

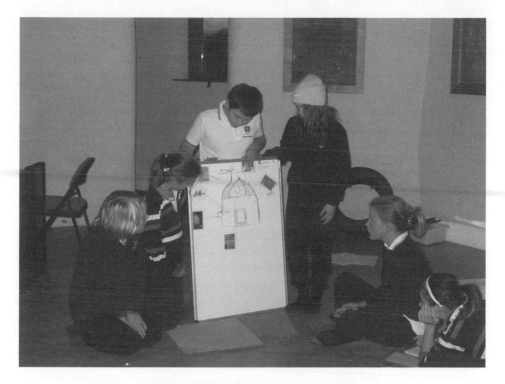

Representing an idea: initial planning (photograph: Belinda Fear)

Artwork to promote water conservation (photograph: Jac Scott)

- during the original visit, in choosing materials, questions began to be raised concerning choice of the 'best' material
- during the artwork in choosing the best way to represent an idea
- choices during the auditing of the schools' energy and water consumption
- choices at the end of phase one in deciding what aspects of the findings to act upon.

From knowing nothing, or very little, about what makes a building, this progressed from the how and the why of buildings to 'What makes a good building?' in work at Goodly Dale. The implications are perhaps that the focus on the concept, the 'big idea', enabled progression to take place.

One characteristic of a long-term plan (meaning longer than a teaching term) is the difficulty of ensuring that objectives meet developing needs. In terms of recent planning practice this may offer a challenge to teachers and schools for a number of reasons, though it is the argument of this chapter, based on the case study, that such challenges can be overcome and can, indeed, enhance the outcomes. In this study a key element of the planning process was a degree of flexibility. It could be argued that it was this flexibility that enabled

Deciding on actions (photograph: Belinda Fear)

the project to be so successful, particularly in its ability to take account of children's interests. By working closely together with The National Trust Community Learning Officer and an artist, it became clear that the second phase of the project needed to be more respon-sive to the individual schools' needs and interests. By letting the project develop more organically it was felt that all parties were more involved with the project as they had more input into its direction and focus.

The planning of a theme like this over 18 months does, however, raise a number of issues and questions which need to be considered.

The challenge of subject choice

Generally certain subjects will naturally 'fit' the theme, but that does not mean that the theme determines the subject. In the case of Goodly Dale School the focus subjects became geography, art and design and technology, while at Elleray the same overall objectives were linked to science, art, ICT and literacy.

While many schools select themes because they offer subject oppor-tunities, the findings of this case study suggest that, at least for long-term projects, the theme can often be imaginatively and successfully linked to a number of subjects.

The challenge of the relationship to both other foundation subjects and to the core subjects

In this case study the three chosen subjects were then expressed in planning terms through a series of 'topics' – materials and architec-ture. This use of smaller topics related and contributing to the overall theme enabled the subject links to be made. Teachers at both Goodly Dale and Elleray, for example, spoke enthusiastically of the increased quality of speaking and listening and questioning they observed. Specifically, Belinda Fear at Elleray spoke of the children's enhanced confidence in speaking because of their enhanced knowledge, their ability to speak without notes due to embedded understanding of the themes they were introducing, and their consequent ability to answer questions from the class. Skills such as these are far more likely from a long-term theme.

The challenge of planning and assessing for learning

It would seem that progression occurred in a series of 'leaps' rather than steadily. An implication of this could be that we need to learn how to identify these 'critical moments' if we are to be successful in assessment for learning. We also need to understand more fully the nature of these 'critical moments'.

Dear Jac and Kelley at the Footprint Project

I am writing to you to thank you for my daughter's involvement with The National Trust Footprint Project. Through Elleray School. Not only has she enjoyed it immensely, but also she has changed our lives and the way that we live. Reduce, Re-use Recycle really are her buzz words.

   If Bethan finds that anyone has put something into the rubbish that could be recycled they are found and told off by Bethan along with reminders on recycling and saving the planet and how we should look after the environment. I am also reprimanded if I forget to reuse my own bags at the supermarket. We have also changed our light bulbs to eco-friendly ones at Bethan's request, as well as composting at home and in the garden.

   I just wanted you to know what a profound effect your project has had not only on Bethan but all 5 members of her immediate family and also the other 16 members of her extended family. (Susannah Cogger, Parent of Bethan at Elleray School)

Figure 8.6   Parent's view on empowerment

Critical moments and the pedagogy of challenging our values

Our observation that children's development in understanding of the key concepts often moved forward in leaps clearly has implications for learning. Peter Woods (1993) used a considerable body of research carried out in the 1980s and early 1990s (Bonnett, 1991). This research identifies what Wood refers to as 'real learning'. He defines this as that which builds upon a pupil's own needs and relevancies, and on their existing cognitive and affective structures. In developing his model of 'real learning', Woods identifies a key process as the handover of control of learning from the teacher to the pupil, a process in which the pupil ceases to learn 'for the teacher' but instead begins to learn 'for themselves'. He identifies this as being both central and radical rather than peripheral and cosmetic. It is a process which changes and empowers the learner.

   Critical events are not the stuff of everyday schooling. They do not always 'just happen' either (although that is indeed possible, and I suspect that most of us can remember those eureka moments, perhaps on the fingers of one hand, from our years at school and out of school). Woods (1993: 10) identifies certain conditions for critical events to occur. He argues that;

- They are usually supported by a whole-school policy. The context is particularly important to the pupils. (In this project the building provided the context, although in addition the need to present and spread the information made the context more real.)
- Different 'rules' may apply (to different children and to different contexts?). Indeed, some would argue (Reimer, 1971) that such events cannot easily happen in schools due to the structures that schools place in their way.

Examples from the case study which promoted opportunities for such events included:

This was largely a 'paper free' theme leading to very different 'rules' in terms of outputs

   The 'critical agent' was provided by both those involved from The National Trust and from the artist.

   The building itself offered what Woods refers to as the 'critical agent' as it raised so many questions which did not have clear answers (see below)

   There were opportunities for older children to teach younger children what they had learnt earlier in the project.

   Children were frequently given choices and opportunities to make judgements, offering the democratic style that Woods identifies.

Figure 8.7 Examples for this project that illustrated Woods' 'Critical Events'

- They all require a 'critical agent', someone who is going to challenge preconceptions.
- They need a democratic management style in the classroom.

The structure of critical events is, then, an important process to understand if we wish to influence not only the learning process but also the values that children develop. Woods (1993: 8) identifies the following suggested structure of critical events:

1 Conceptualization. In terms of this case study this took the form of the visit to the site prior to construction. Children were challenged not only with the design but also with the issues surrounding The National Trust's decision to build a learning base using innovative techniques and materials. Particularly important was the opportunity to clarify key concepts, in this case those surrounding sustainability, early in the project. In clarifying the term 'sustainability', Anna, Grania, Evie and Ben of Elleray School; (To make sure important and valuable resources don't run out in the near future) were demonstrating an initial understanding.

2 Preparation and planning. The skills needed for involvement in this project covered a range of subject areas, from science (in understanding the properties of different materials) to geography (the choice of site for the building and the environmental implications of different choices) and art in the creative approaches to expressing ideas. A characteristic of the feedback on this project was the significance of children's involvement in the planning process.

3 Divergence. In the St Catherine's case study this stage came later than the model would predict. Indeed, according to the teacher, it would seem that it was the final visit to an eco-project that stimulated the children to diverge in their thinking. It was the recognition, while on this visit, that the answers to the questions were not quite as straightforward as they thought. Perhaps a wind turbine was

not the simple solution to the school's energy needs that they had hoped it would be. In the case of Elleray there was a clear 'moment of understanding' when they were shown the digital display board that shows energy inputs and outputs in real time.

4 Convergence. Woods identifies this as a process of discarding as well as selecting. At St Catherine's, convergence appeared to be happening as the children designed their approach to engaging others in the environmental changes that they wished to see around their school. They had to select, discard and prioritize to do this. It is significant that not all children reach this stage, and certainly in this project the different levels of understanding became clear. At Elleray 'integration' appeared when children applied their understanding to later work on food miles.

5 Consolidation. At Goodly Dale this occurred while the children were designing their own buildings in an architecture topic during the final term of the project. Here they had to bring together the wide variety of thoughts and skills that had been developed over the previous 12 months.

6 Celebration. Assembly presentations to parents and others involved secured the celebration of their work. At Elleray the children produced games for parents and all children were involved in producing a variety of PowerPoint presentations on the theme. (See WM 8.2.) An example of a song used in one of these presentations can be seen in Figure 8.11 near the end of this chapter.

If indeed 'critical moments' were inspired by this long-term partnership then we could liken them to what Nottingham (2008, 2009) refers to as 'eureka' moments in his discussion of the 'learning pit'. At Goodly Dale, Philosophy for Children was used as a strategy on a number of occasions to introduce the children to the tensions that inevitably underlie an environmental building project such as this. James Nottingham uses his discussion of the 'learning pit' to identify tensions between possible solutions as being a key way by which we learn to challenge our own and others' thinking.

In this theme a visit to the new building 16 months into the theme was set up to 'meet the builder' and to raise questions about the new structure. These questions were not in themselves philosophical, as one would hope for a philosophy for children session. They did, however, illustrate that many of the children had begun to recognize tensions over decisions that had been made. It would be argued by both Woods and Nottingham, I suspect, that these tensions are the second stage in developing those new visions of our understanding that lead to 'eureka' moments.

Figure 8.9 shows how this might have happened in this project. The first and last column represents responses from children to questioning

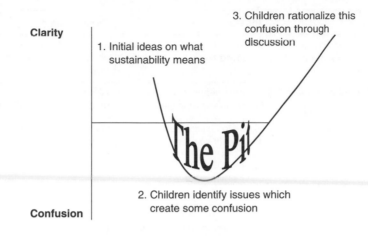

Figure 8.8 The Learning Pit (Nottingham, 2008, 2009)

sessions a year apart. The first, in June 2007, took place at the Footprint building and involved a teacher in role as the builder. The children, invited to ask questions, clearly focused on pragmatic areas of interest. The questions were wide-ranging, but on the whole required answers which identified some of the tensions embodied in trying to make a building 'sustainable'. The last column represents the outcomes from a session exploring the meaning of sustainability and took place a year later. Here the children's questions have clearly matured, identifying some very complex and difficult aspects of the idea of sustainability. It is clear that these children have continued to develop their philosophical reasoning through 'philosophy for children', but in addition it appears that the tensions raised by the meet-the-builder session a year earlier, together with continuing reflection on the ideas over the year, has enabled them to verbalize their questions in more sophisticated ways.

Interestingly, the children's ability to move through these tensions became more rapid. While initially children at Elleray were struck by the conflict raised by visiting an eco-centre by bus, their later work on food miles, where they rapidly identified the tension between buying local food and our existing reliance on food which travels large distances, showed greater sophistication in analysis. There appear to be stages through which we all go in our ability to spot tensions such as these.

Learning styles, creativity and inclusion

It is interesting that, in reviewing this case study, children fairly consistently valued the hands-on aspects of the partnership. The teacher identified this as being distinct from the 'creative' aspects, involving learning

Initial idea	Tension	Final thought
June 2006 Question asked in a meet the 'builder' teacher-in-role session	Reflection on the tension resulting from the 'builder's' answer	June 2007 in a discussion about the meaning of sustainability
Where did the straw come from?	*But that means it was transported a long way*	Why should people use resources carefully? Ellie
Is what you have done good for the environment or are there bad things as well?	*Maybe there is no such thing as the perfect solution?*	How much can we reduce our negative impact without damaging our life style? Aaron
How long will the building last?	*Does anything last?*	Could something ever last forever? Carrie
Could we build all buildings out of straw?	*Is there only one solution to these problems? Can everyone expect the same lifestyle?*	How can you share anything equally?

Figure 8.9   Development of thinking through facing up to the implications of tensions over a period of one year

skills in manipulating material, for example. Since most of the work was carried out in groups, co-operation became the heart of inclusion. Children could select the tasks that they were most able to achieve. In making signs, for example, some children focused on the artwork, some on the message and others on the practical aspects. Creativity developed from the structured yet open approach, an example of which can be seen in the poster design task again. Children were given a design brief in which a human shape needed to 'represent' the message in some way. The children had to bring in their own materials from home, so the 'save electricity' poster included cable, the 'recycle' poster plastic bags, the 'save water' poster pool tiles, and so on.

While creativity played an important part in this case study it is clear that it took many forms. Apart from the obviously creative work in engaging with the art, children were consistently asked to be creative in their thinking, particularly through the use of philosophical enquiry in the classroom.

Creativity is perhaps often associated with cross-curricular learning but there is little research which directly identifies higher levels of creativity in an integrated curriculum. It clearly depends upon how one defines creativity.

Values development

It is often argued (see Bloom's taxonomy, more recently reviewed in Anderson et al., 2001) that action is most likely when children have

Creative artwork to promote water conservation (photograph: Jac Scott)

experienced structured opportunities to internalize new values. This ability to internalize comes from a sequential development, beginning with awareness through to establishment of a life outlook. Rokeach (1973) argued that the cognitive and the affective are essential to this internalization process. This project raised tensions by expressing a lack of certainty, and it is likely that this will have influenced values more than a project which gave simplistic answers to the questions raised by such a building.

In the case of environmental education there are many dispositions which might be considered as desirable in developing an action orientation. Two in particular seem to have become evident in this case study:

- Delayed gratification. This is the idea that we will have to wait for periods of time to see the results of any action that we take. At its simplest level we would expect to see children recognizing that sowing a seed to grow food may involve acting several months prior to harvesting. On a more complex level, we would be looking for recognition that we may need to sacrifice something in the shorter term if we wish to see a greater good in the longer term. In the St Catherine's example there is evidence that this was beginning to happen, almost certainly the result of the project being long term.
- Recognition of intrinsic worth. This is the notion that something has a value *in itself*, regardless of any benefits that we might have from it. An

The Footprint Project started in Year 4. On the day we started we were learning about sustainability and what things are sustainable. When we moved into Year 5 that was when everything was happening: the footprint was being finished, we were making a nest out of wool, making felt with our feet. When we moved into Year 6 we started to focus on how we could save energy and the world, these are some of the ideas we came up with: turning off lights when they're not being used, using our legs instead of using cars, take less baths and more showers, put water-saving facilities in the toilets. In the future I hope the world will be a better place to live in.
(Hannah Clark)

Figure 8.10   An illustration of delayed gratification

example might be recognition that preserving a landscape or just a tree is a worthwhile thing to do even though there is no evident personal advantage to doing that. In order to evaluate their engagement with this concept the children at Elleray discussed types of 'worth' after the project. They managed to identify: ability to buy things (purchasing); how useful something is to us (utility); to all of us in our country or community (culture); to our well-being (family, love, sentimental and spiritual); knowledge and understanding (educational); skills (in somebody's ability to do or make something). After this discussion children ranked pictures of a family, a tree, the globe, money, a car, pets, a sculpture, a view and a wasp in different ways, depending on what they saw as the 'worth' of each. The results indicated a clear empathy with environment together with, as one would expect, a recognition of the worth of a family. Most interesting, however, was the discussion surrounding the activity in which children talked, on several occasions, about a concept that they referred to as 'just worth', apparently meaning that some things can hold worth irrespective of utility or, indeed, any of the types of worth that we had discussed before the activity. Have these children begun to develop a more deep-rooted idea that some things cannot be measured in the traditional ways that we, as humans, see worth? Other possible examples of this development can be seen in the numerous occasions that children recognized the environment as a 'special place' worthy of preservation for its own sake (discussion with Kelley Sproston, The National Trust Learning Officer responsible for the partnership). Actions included, conserving water, travelling less, saving energy and recycling. Each of these actions include elements of both delayed gratification and recognition of intrinsic worth.

Conclusion

One of the biggest challenges of long-term projects such as this is the difficulty of replication. The initial stimulus and essential context are now complete, so how do we repeat something as powerful as this with

> Your place, is our place,
> it's nothing very fancy Sir I know,
> but it's all that I have got,
> so I'm asking you to stop
> cos there is really nowhere else that I can go,
> no there is really nowhere else that I can go.
> Your trees are our trees,
> they're nothing very fancy Sir we know,
> but it's all that we have got,
> so we're asking you to stop
> 'coz there is really nowhere else that we can go, no there is really nowhere else that we can go.
> Your world is our world,
> it's nothing very fancy Sir we know,
> but it's all that we have got,
> so we are asking you to stop
> 'coz there is really no where else that we can go, no there is really nowhere else that we can go.

Figure 8.11 Song written by children of Elleray School at the conclusion of the project

the next year group? This is a challenge that all schools face in trying to develop these long-term learning objectives. The Footprint Project, however, has identified certain pointers to help identify the way in which long-term cross-curricular projects can enhance development of values relating to the environment.

1 Consider how the stages proposed by Woods (1993) might influence your planning.
2 Look for opportunities to identify tensions and remember that the initial confusion that these create can often lead to clearer learning (the learning pit).
3 Identify a key point at which children can take more ownership of the learning and have structured opportunities to influence its direction.
4 Develop a strong connection with a place by visiting it on a number of occasions and identify changes that are taking place.

References

Anderson, L.W. et. al. (eds) (2001) *A Taxonomy for Learning, Teaching, and Assessing: A Revision of Bloom's Taxonomy of Educational Objectives*. New York: Longman.

Bonnett, M. (1991) 'Developing children's thinking', *Cambridge Journal of Education*, 2 (3): 249–58.

Bonnett, M. (2004) *Retrieving Nature: Education for a Post-humanist Age*. Oxford: Blackwell.

Hattie, J. (2003) 'Teachers make a difference: what is the research evidence?', Australian Council for Educational Research Annual Conference on Building Teacher Quality.

Nottingham, J. (2008) Sustained Success. Available: www.sustained-success.com [2008, April 2008] .

Nottingham, J. (2009) '*Learning to Succeed: the FACTS*'. Wakefield: Teaching and Learning Publications.

Orr, D.W. (2004) *Earth in Mind: On Education, Environment, and the Human Prospect*. 10th anniversary edn. Washington, DC: Island.

Palmer, J. and Wise, M. (1982) *Good, the Bad and the Ugly*. Sheffield: Geographical Association.

Reimer, E. (1971) *School Is Dead: An Essay on Alternatives in Education*. Harmondsworth: Penguin.

Rokeach, M. (1973) *The Nature of Human Values*. London: Collier Macmillan.

Sterling, S.R. and Schumacher Society (2001) *Sustainable Education: Re-visioning Learning and Change*. Totnes: Green Books for the Schumacher Society.

Woods, P. (1993) *Critical Events in Teaching and Learning*. London: Falmer.

What it means for primary-aged children to be internationally minded: the contribution of geography and history

Martin Skelton and Graham Reeves

Chapter introduction

This chapter looks at the development of international-mindedness in young children, particularly through the contributions made by history and geography. It begins by looking at what it is to learn and at the implications of that for cross-curricular learning, and then looks more closely at what it is to learn history and geography. The chapter then looks at a definition of international-mindedness and the issues of that definition for primary children and their teachers. It then considers the contribution history and geography can make to the development of international-mindedness. Throughout the chapter, two case studies from schools using the International Primary Curriculum are used to illustrate the approach. (Sheryl Wrigley is Deputy Head Teacher at St Aloysius Catholic Primary School in Huyton, Knowsley and Vicky Sewell is a Year 2 Teacher at Christ Church Church of England Primary School in Ellesmere Port, Cheshire.)

The International Primary Curriculum

The International Primary Curriculum (Skelton et al., 2004) was originally developed for a group of around 15 primary schools situated in various parts of the world, mostly in fairly remote locations. The schools were populated mainly by expatriate children from an increasingly wide range of countries. The schools had decided that their existing curricula no longer met the needs of their culturally diverse rolls and were looking for something different. They could not find what they were looking for so Fieldwork Education, an organization based in the UK but with considerable experience of working with schools worldwide, was commissioned to produce it for them. Interest in this new curriculum quickly spread to other schools and, from the original small group that began implementing the IPC in 2001, by 2008 there were over 500 schools using it – in more than 50 countries. Use is no longer limited to international schools; the IPC has also been adopted by national schools – many of them in the UK but also in the Netherlands, Germany, Kenya, Malaysia and Indonesia.

The IPC draws heavily on what has been learned from the recent brain research previously discussed, and particularly on the theory of multiple intelligences devised by Professor Howard Gardner (2006). It covers the full range of primary school subjects. For each subject there is a set of 'learning goals' that define what children are expected to learn by the time they are 7, 9 and 12 years old – also known as Mileposts 1, 2 and 3. The IPC also includes a considerable number of thematic and interdisciplinary 'units of work' through which teachers can help children achieve the learning goals.

As well as the main IPC programme there is also an Early Years programme, an Assessment for Learning programme and an online 'Members' Lounge' where schools and teachers exchange ideas and suggestions within a global network. More information about the International Primary Curriculum can be found at WL 9.1 and further case studies can be found at WL 9.2.

One of the recurring themes of the IPC is that of 'independence and interdependence'. Another is connections. These have a great deal of relevance to curriculum subjects. Each subject is regarded as independent, which is why each one has its own learning goals. The subjects are also regarded as interdependent – which explains the importance of the units of work. Children are taught to make connections, not just within the subjects but also between them in order to consolidate their learning.

Children learning?

Most of us in education do not focus on learning as much as we should. We often pay lip-service to 'learning' but the evidence of our actions points elsewhere. It points to teaching, which is why we observe teachers in the classroom, look at teachers' plans, and report back on the 'quality of teaching'. It points to curriculum, which is why we spend so much time writing curriculum plans for the school and lesson plans for

Where our food comes from

our classrooms. It points to management, which is why we find ourselves with teachers who are given responsibility for subject co-ordination across the whole school. It points to professional development, which is why we go on courses, read books and, occasionally, visit other colleagues. It points to resources, which is why we order books and films and subscribe to online resource banks.

All these things are important and all of them make a contribution. But none of them focus on learning. We are slowly coming to realize that a well-planned lesson, based on a well-articulated curriculum, overseen by a well-intentioned and well-qualified subject manager, supported by the appropriate resources, does not guarantee learning. It is true that having the evidence that these things are all in place might increase the chance that learning is happening. But they do not guarantee it.

The way to know whether learning is taking place is twofold. First, we need to define what learning is; second, we need to look for it in the classroom. We are going to begin by attempting a definition of what is going on when children are learning. It is a definition in four parts, all of which have been developed in our work with children, teachers and schools over the past 20 years and, more specifically, over the past seven years.

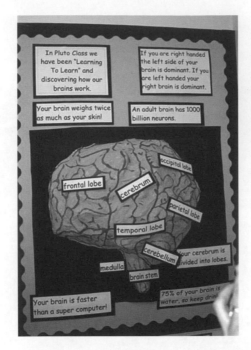

Brain display

Part 1: Connections

The explosion in brain research has been both a help and a hindrance to teachers over the past 20 years. It has been a hindrance because many of us have been beguiled into adopting classroom practices that are largely unproven. It has been a help because some aspects of brain research have been shown to have transference from animals to humans and from the laboratory to the classroom.

One example of the latter is the research into the behaviour of neurons. Neurons are the building blocks of the brain and of learning. Research has shown us that neurons are hard-wired or programmed to behave in particular ways. Put simply, as each neuron is 'turned on' by one stimulus or another, it sends out an electrical-chemical messenger that tries to connect with another neuron. The more often this connection between specific neurons is made the more it automatically occurs. (This can be a good or bad thing. As brain researchers say, practice makes permanent, not perfect.)

We have around 100 billion neurons which means that the number of potential connections between them is incalculable; it is a huge amount. As we grow from our time in the womb to adulthood and beyond, the simple connections of a few neurons made in our very early days of life become enormously complex webs of constellations of neurons as we grow older.

'Through everything that we do with the IPC there are connections; connections with other countries, connections with other subjects, connections with past units and, as a result, the children are more engaged in everything that they do and more open-minded to their learning and to our place in the world. These children haven't been taught through isolated subjects; since starting school their learning about geography and history as well as all the other foundation subjects has been thematic with lots and lots of connections and it's very apparent in the way they think and view things. And all these connections have had a strong international focus. I can see the difference in these children as a result of that. They may still have prejudices from family and local society influences, but I think we are promoting a lot of cultural respect and understanding because of the IPC.'
(Vicky Sewell, Christ Church Church of England Primary School, Ellesmere Port, Cheshire)

Figure 9.1   Local connections

The research into neuronal behaviour has made legitimate what many teachers have suspected about learning. It is a matter of connection. Learning does not really happen unless whatever is currently being learned can be connected to what has previously been learned.

This issue of connections is a vital one, with two important implications. First, from the earliest stage of development, the programmed neuronal behaviour is based on each neuron making a connection with another neuron. The brain automatically tries to make this happen. For example, when we visit a new town most of us find ourselves 'automatically' saying 'This town reminds me of … ' another town that we have been to. Or when we see a newborn baby in the family we frequently say 'Doesn't she look like Auntie X'. It's almost impossible not to do this; it is a visible indication of the brain's programmed desire to make connections.

This is why using analogies and metaphor is so powerful in helping learners. Sentences such as 'I know you are struggling with this at the moment, but imagine that it's like a …' help the learner's brain to begin to get a sense of what the subject matter is about.

Implications for cross-curricular learning

As the constellations of neurons grow larger and more complex, the same simple connections continue to happen but another set of connections also comes into play. The growing density and complexity of our neuronal network enables connections to be made across subjects or fields of knowledge and not just within them. In fact, as we make our own definitions of people who are 'bright' or 'intelligent' we may refer to a density of connections in one subject but we are just as likely to refer to a density of connections across subjects. Christiano Ronaldo would be an example of the former. No one can deny that he has a complex web of connections within the kinaesthetic field. Stephen Fry might be an example of the latter; someone who is able to talk about a novel he has written but then almost simultaneously find its connection within the fields of art and music.

This ability to make broader and broader connections is both a marker of extended learning (because it enables a multi-perspective view to emerge) and a help to the learning process itself (because the more pathways that exist to what it is we need to recall the more chances we have to recall it).

Through her use of the International Primary Curriculum with her children (Figure 9.1) Vicky Sewell is demonstrating how curriculum planning can mirror the potential behaviour of the brain. The subject – science, art, geography – now takes a co-starring role in her planning alongside the theme that is being studied. Through the rigorous planning of the IPC and her own classroom, planning around a theme that interests children, she is able to help them see each subject as both important in its own right and as a contributor to a much broader awareness of an issue. This is at the heart of cross-curriculum planning. For it to be worthwhile, it must have a purpose related to children's learning rather than to preferred methods of classroom learning.

New learning, consolidated learning, drowning and treading water

Learning happens when we make connections. But it happens in four different ways.

New learning happens when the connections are first being made. By definition this learning is a struggle. It is insecure; we all need support and scaffolding at this time. ('I'm beginning to be able to find north using this compass but I often get it wrong.')

Consolidated learning is the result of practice and the revisiting of this new learning. Consolidation is a time of increasing security and greater confidence. ('If you need help to find north on the compass just ask me. I finally cracked it last week.')

Drowning is when the learning process is interrupted and starts to fail. In the drowning phase, that which we thought was becoming secure and consolidated starts to unravel. Drowning is a struggle too but, unlike new learning, the struggle is a negative and disheartening one. ('I thought I was getting how to find north but since you asked me to do it differently it's all gone wonky again.')

Treading water looks like learning but is not really. Treading water is activity that is being undertaken for no real learning purpose. The activity is not creating new or consolidated learning. When we are in the process of treading water we are just going through the motions. ('Why am I doing these "finding north" activities lesson after lesson? I know some people still can't do it but I've got it right every time for the past three weeks.')

Building a volcano

Part 2: Knowledge, skills and understanding

As we make connections successfully (new or consolidated), unsuccess-fully (drowning) or not (treading water) we make them in three increas-ingly complex kinds of learning.

Knowledge (knowing 'that') is factual

Knowledge is the collection of information that, for now, we all agree to be true. (Paris *is* the capital of France.) Knowledge is right or wrong. It is the most easily assessable; group tests will do a very good job. The problem with knowledge is its exponential expansion, in which current estimates indicate that by 2010 the amount of knowledge in the world – fuelled by more researchers, better technology and enhanced research methods – will double every 80 or so days. This means that we are faced with having to select what of the available knowledge it is appropriate to teach to children at what stage; we simply cannot teach it all. Our view is that we need to teach children three kinds of knowledge – *essential knowledge* (that which children must know), *motivational knowledge* (that which excites children; what a friend used to call 'Gee Whiz! Knowledge'), and *transformational knowledge* (that which is not essential but causes children to think in a more expanded way).

'As for geography, our children have, until very recently, had very little understanding outside their own area of Huyton. We've recently completed the IPC Airports unit and it has been an excellent unit for helping the children to understand the process of travelling abroad. In this, and many other IPC units, the children are applying their knowledge of places in the world – such as countries, continents and hemispheres – to their developing geographical skills such as map reading and map making. This combination of knowledge and skills is a natural part of every IPC unit and because it's put into the context of the topic that the children are learning, it makes sense to them. This is inspiring some of our children – and sometimes the ones you least expect – to find out more at home, wanting to do their own research and coming back into school saying things like "did you know ..." It's amazing, the change we're seeing.'
(Sheryl Wrigley is Deputy Head Teacher at St Aloysius Catholic Primary School in Huyton, Knowsley)

Figure 9.2   Airports

Knowledge of history and geography

Knowledge, as we have said, is concerned with information – with facts. At first sight knowledge, as it relates to history and geography, is not problematic. It is relatively easy to teach. If I want children to know that, say, Berlin is the capital of Germany, I can tell them. Then they have the knowledge. To reinforce the knowledge, I can tell them again, I can get them to search the Internet, I can tell them to read about it, I can display posters and maps and arrange all sorts of activities so that the knowledge becomes embedded. Knowledge is relatively easy to assess as well. If I want to find out whether the children know that Berlin is the capital of Germany, I can ask them. If I want to be sure, I can vary the questions: 'What is the capital of Germany?', 'Of which country is Berlin the capital?' The children know and I know that they know.

The real dilemma is in identifying which facts the children should know. There are so many of them. And every moment there are more and more.

Determining the historical and geographical facts that children should know involves all sorts of choices. Decisions are taken on cultural, social, political and pragmatic grounds – and on custom and practice. Is there any real reason why primary school children in England should learn about the Ancient Egyptians rather than, say, the Ancient Persians? The Victorians rather than the Georgians? Britain since 1930 rather than Britain since 1910? The Ancient Greeks rather than the Visigoths?

Let us not pretend that there is anything sacred about what someone has decided children should learn about. They have to learn about something and what has been decided is as good as anything else. It is right that children learn about the past and about places. It is particularly important that they learn about their heritage – facts related to the country in which most of them were born. But, in reality, the decisions are arbitrary. And, for the moment, we are not even touching on issues

Understanding history

about why, in history, dates and events relating to 'famous people' are more important than those relating to others. Nor have we mentioned the fact that, although they may be living in the UK, many children also have a heritage that includes countries other than the UK.

Facts are an important part of the study of history and geography but facts are more problematic than some would have us believe.

The IPC does not claim to have the final answer to all the issues about how to choose the facts that children should learn about. But it does take a different line from that of most programmes. Taking a thematic approach and one originally designed for international schools catering for expatriates, it adopts a principle about history and geography that also applies to art, music and other subjects. This approach is summed up in the words 'host country, home country'. So, when working on a theme of 'Explorers and adventurers', for example, children will learn about explorers and adventurers from and of the country where they are living and about explorers and adventurers from the country that they might call 'home'. Schools in national systems that have adopted the IPC have generally adapted the approach so that children learn not only about the history and geography of the country in which they are living, but also about at least one other country.

This approach of 'home' and 'host' is an important one in the development of ideas about history, geography and international-mindedness. Underpinning it is the view that at all times children should be enabled

'The home and host country approach with the IPC also means that we're always looking at a theme, not just from our own local perspective, but also from that of another country. With the Airports unit our host country was Spain. In our foundation stage the children are presently learning through the IPC theme "Treasure" and their "host country" is Jamaica. We're trying to make our home countries relevant for the unit or personal to the teacher's travel experiences (the children respond very well to hearing about and seeing their teacher in real-life situations), or personal to one or some of the children in the class'.
(Sheryl Wrigley is Deputy Head Teacher at St Aloysius Catholic Primary School in Huyton, Knowsley)

Figure 9.3   Home and host country

to begin to develop a multi-perspective view, an issue both of skills and values development. It does not subjugate any particular national view-point but neither does it raise it up as pre-eminent either.

Such an approach is not a simple one, particularly in classes where there are children from many different nationalities. But history and geography are not simple, whatever curriculum is used. They are com-plex subjects – and not just because of the issues involved in deciding which facts children should be learning.

One of the problems about facts is that they can change, as situations change and more knowledge is available. How many countries are in the European Union? What is Yugoslavia? How high is Mount Everest? Why did the Vikings invade Britain? The 'factual' answers given to each of these questions now would be different from those that would have been accepted a few years ago.

Skills (knowing 'how') are practical
Skills range from 'I am able to put my key in the key lock' to 'I am able to diagnose a brain tumour'. What binds all skills together is that they are active. Although there are many skills we use in the world (typing this chapter is another) the good news about skills in school subjects is that they are few and change less frequently than knowledge. The tech-nology may have advanced but what historians or geographers actually do changes very slowly. A key difference between skills and knowledge, though, is that skills have to be assessed in action. ('I can only tell whether you can read coordinates by observing you do it.')

Skills in history and geography
It is partly – but not entirely – because of the problem of knowledge that skills are so important in history and geography. With the number of facts increasing so rapidly and with the facts changing, people (and not just those people who happen, at the moment, to be children) need to know how to find things out and how to test the reliability of information. In addition, children who have found information for themselves are more

likely to remember it. In short, we have to teach children the process of enquiry in history, geography or, indeed, any other subject. That means that we have to have an idea of what it means to be a historian or a geographer at, say, the age of 7, 9 or 11 years.

The first challenge though, as we have already said, is that skills and the development of understanding are not as easy to teach as facts. If we think that it is a historical fact that they should know, we can tell children that Henry VIII had six wives and, with sufficient reinforcement, they will know it. It is not quite as straightforward to tell them how to conduct a historical investigation and assume that they will know how to do it. And when it comes to assessment, we can very easily ask children 'How many wives did Henry VIII have?' and find out whether or not they know. We cannot ask 'Do you know how to conduct a historical investigation?' and expect to gather some reliable assessment evidence. Children need to practise the skills relevant to history and geography in order to learn them and to accurately assess them we need to observe children in order to know whether they have learned the skills.

In the IPC, the history and geography skills that primary school children are expected to learn are summarized as:

- finding out about the past
- finding out about places and environments
- interpreting information
- presenting their work.

These big-picture descriptions are expressed in more detail in the learning goals for each milepost. At Milepost 1 (the end of the school year in which children are 7), for example, children are expected to be able to:

- use geographical terms
- follow directions
- describe the geographical features of the school site and other familiar places
- make maps and plans of real and imaginary places, using pictures and symbols
- use maps at a variety of scales to locate the position and simple geographical features of the host country and their home country
- use secondary sources to obtain simple geographical information
- express views on the attractive and unattractive features of an environment
- communicate their geographical knowledge and understanding in a variety of ways.

Skills relevant to geography and history are here being successfully introduced at a very young age and their strong connections to

'I can see already what an impact the IPC has had on Year 2 children, and each new IPC unit is building on the knowledge, skills and understanding that they've already developed from previous units. You don't just teach something from a local perspective. Everything you do is very much linked to other countries around the world. As a result of this, the children have already become familiar with world maps and how to use them. The IPC teaches them the skills to find out more and to get more involved in what they're learning. For example the children all love using Google Earth. We've looked at how small our country is compared to the whole world. Google Earth is excellent for reflecting the whole world as one large community without centralizing the UK, and helps us with all our host and home country work.'
(Vicky Sewell is Year 2 Teacher at Christ Church Church of England Primary School in Ellesmere Port, Cheshire)

Figure 9.4   Google Earth

the theme are ensuring that children are constantly applying these skills; progressing them quite rapidly from 'beginning' to 'developing' levels. As we have said, these skills are not as easy to teach as the facts. But, put into the context of the theme, as Vicky has experienced, the opportunities for beginning and then developing those skills, such as map reading or being able to give reasons for particular changes in history, are plentiful. Not only that, but they are clearly interesting and/or fun for the children because there is meaning to what they are doing, resulting in engagement, resulting in even more learning.

This is an indication of how the IPC would set out what it means to be a geographer at the age of 7. The learning goals are expressed as more specific 'learning goals' in the various units of work. Then the IPC Assessment for Learning programme takes things further by articulating 'rubrics' for each learning goal. So, for the learning goal about children being 'able to use maps at a variety of scales to locate the position and simple geographical features of the host country and their home country', there is a rubric describing what this actually means at three different levels: beginning, developing and mastering.

The skills-related learning goals for history at Milepost 2 (the end of the school year in which children are 9) include stating that children are expected to be able to:

- give some reasons for particular events and changes
- gather information from simple sources
- use their knowledge and understanding to answer simple questions about the past and about changes.

Again, these are made more specific in the learning targets contained in units of work and then supported by assessment rubrics:

Beginning	The child can draw a simple map or plan of a real or imaginary place with basic features that he/she can identify verbally with help from the teacher.	When making a map of a real place, the features are not in their corrrect relative positions.	There is no key.
Developing	The child can make a simple map or plan of a real or imaginary place with some identifiable features in pictorial form.	When making a map of a real place the features are not all in their correct relative positions.	There is no key.
Mastering	The child independently produces a map or plan of a real or imaginary place with three or more identifiable features in their correct relative positions.	Features may be shown as pictures or symbols.	There is a form of key.

Figure 9.5   IPC progression in mapwork

Beginning	Developing	Mastering
The child uses one or more simple sources to answer predetermined questions. The child needs assistance in choosing the relevant source and to locate the answers from it.	The child uses a few sources with some degree of confidence and ease to locate the answers to research questions. The child may have devised some of these questions him/herself.	The child uses a range of sources to answer many questions set by the teacher and him/herself. The child has a good idea as to the usefulness of each source and uses them appropriately.

Figure 9.6   IPC progression in history

Understanding (knowing 'why') is far more complex than either knowledge or skills

The problem with understanding is that we confuse the way we use it in ordinary conversation with what it actually means in terms of learning. Understanding involves a combination of accumulated knowledge, practised skills and reflection over time – and even then it is not anywhere near as possible to facilitate as knowledge or skills. It is also much more difficult to assess. Assessing knowledge requires little judgement; assessing skills requires some judgement; assessing understanding is all about judgement.

In Figure 9.7 Vicky Sewell raises at least two interesting questions. What is being learned? At what age is it appropriate to introduce rigorous ideas about international-mindedness? Our view is that young children, and certainly those in Years 1 and 2, are only beginning to be at the stage where an awareness of the content and values implicit in

'Last year, Years 1 and 2 spent six weeks working on the IPC Places People Go unit. As our entry point to launch the unit to the children we went on a pretend holiday to Spain. This included all the preparation for the journey, including making passports, tickets and luggage tags, and then going on the journey! We set up one classroom as a check-in desk and each child had to check in with their luggage they'd brought from home and their pretend ticket and passport. There was some excellent role play including asking them all the questions they would normally be asked at an airport. We set up another classroom as a plane with the appropriate seating and aisles, the white board was a flight simulator, the adults were the crew, and the passengers ate their dinners out of tin foil trays! When the children arrived in Spain they did lots of Spanish activities including eating tapas, enjoying a siesta and going to the beach. It helped to create a complete experience of flying somewhere for a holiday as well as highlighting some of the cultural differences between England and Spain. The role play was unbelievable. More than half of the children had never experienced being on a plane before but afterwards they all talked about it as if they'd experienced it for real.'
(Vicky Sewell, Christ Church Church of England Primary School, Ellesmere Port, Cheshire)

Figure 9.7   A pretend holiday in Spain

international-mindedness can be usefully introduced. Those children are building their knowledge about similarities and differences between different cultures and, at a beginning level, developing the important cross-cultural skill of seeing the 'other' as different rather than wrong.

Understanding history and geography

Being a historian, whether in primary school, secondary school, university or beyond, requires knowledge and skills. It also requires understanding.

As outlined at the beginning of the chapter, if the skills of history and geography are more difficult and time-consuming to teach and assess than the knowledge, understanding is more difficult again. We have described how it requires a great deal more than telling, and a great deal more than practice – and it cannot be assessed through a simple test. In the IPC, the learning goals and targets that begin 'children will understand … ' are recognized as shorthand for 'children will develop an understanding of … '. For Milepost 3 (the end of the school year in which children are 12), for example, there is a learning goal that says that children are expected to 'understand how localities are affected by natural features and processes'. There is a real question about the extent to which an 11- or 12-year-old – or most adults, for that matter – can really understand that. If we take the fuller version, 'children will develop an understanding of how localities are affected by natural features and processes', there's a greater chance of success. If we changed the goal to read 'children will know that … ', then that is certainly possible. But knowledge – important as it is – is not enough. History, geography, and all the other subjects, require understanding as well as knowledge and skills. That understanding does not come easily but the developmental process can start with young children so that they can begin to see that history and geography are about more than learning facts and how to do certain things.

The beginnings of understanding make it possible for children to start to see the significance of history and geography. Among the things that the IPC says that children should be taught about are:

- in history – how their own lives are affected by historical influences, and
- in geography – how their own lives, and those of other people, are affected by geographical and environmental factors.

The notion is that both subjects are relevant to their own lives. The knowledge that they accumulate will help them to see that. The skills will mean that they can do things that will help them to identify the connections. It is through developing understanding that they will begin to recognize the relevance. That recognition will contribute to making their learning meaningful and enable them to move towards achieving the IPC Personal Goals which describe the personal qualities of enquiry, adaptability, resilience, morality, communication, thoughtfulness, cooperation and respect.

Introducing the learning of history and geography within a theme from a personal or local – 'self' – perspective is allowing a primary-age child to begin their learning egocentrically, in a place that they are familiar and comfortable with. Using this personal perspective to then directly connect to an international – 'other' – perspective is helping to introduce that understanding of international-mindedness. Sheryl's recounting of the clothing exercise in Figure 9.8 is a good example of where this works well.

Part 3: Beginning, developing, mastering

By identifying learning in all subjects, we are now able to identify whether children are learning knowledge, skills or understanding and whether that learning is new, consolidated, drowning or treading water.

There is one other differentiation of learning we need to consider that is particularly relevant to skills. If knowledge learning is on or off, right or wrong, then skills learning is developmental. Skills learning always moves through the three stages of beginning, developing and mastering. That is why ski slopes are defined as green, blue and black. It is true in knowledge terms that a skier on all three pistes is skiing, but we would be better defining the green-piste skier as at the 'beginning' level, the blue-piste skier as at the 'developing' level and

'The geography segments of the IPC units also help me to teach my children about interdependency between countries. For example I did an exercise with my class where they looked at all the clothes they were wearing and where each item came from. It was amazing to them. There wasn't a single item of clothing in the entire class that came from Britain! All the different clothes were made in other countries around the world. I asked the children to think about what they would do if they couldn't get their clothes from these other countries. As a result of this exercise, one of the children then went home and looked at what Britain does produce as a country and came into class the next day with everything he'd learned. This inspired several of the boys to then get involved in looking at where different models of cars are produced. They were all so engaged in the issue; especially a fast-growing realization amongst them all that lots and lots of things around them don't come from Britain; that we need other countries for many of our basic needs. This was a very powerful exercise for the children and one that has made a big difference to their outlook on the world and our place in it.

'Even now, after a very short while with the IPC, there's a changing mindset amongst the children. They are beginning to realize that they are a very small part of a much bigger world community and that everyone, everywhere has a part to play in this community. Our children are definitely more aware of others beyond their immediate world of Huyton. It's a process that takes time but it is definitely changing. I am certain that once the children follow IPC at Foundation Stage to Year 6 there will be enough time to embed a much more internationally minded attitude within all the children. By the time they leave us, these children will have a totally different perspective of the world. I do believe that the IPC's approach to international-mindedness will have a long-term impact into adulthood for them.'

(Sheryl Wrigley is Deputy Head Teacher at St Aloysius Catholic Primary School in Huyton, Knowsley)

Figure 9.8   Clothing

the black-piste skier as at the 'mastering' level. (Even at the mastering level, learners are still involved in a progressive process. There is no doubt that Tiger Woods is a 'mastering' golfer but he still has skills to develop.)

Part 4: Engaging

Finally, we would hope that children are also learning to like learning, and learning to like the subject and its component knowledge, skills and understanding. Generations of children have learned something in school *except* the capacity to want to carry on learning. In our changing world, the ability to learn and the desire to learn are vital dispositions. So we might describe children who develop these dispositions as being engaged by their learning.

We now have a definition of what is happening when children are learning: a combination of knowledge, skills and understanding, passing through – in the case of skills – beginning, developing and mastering stages. At each stage children's learning is potentially new, consolidated, drowning or treading water. Hopefully, children will also be learning to love the process.

Skills, 'knowing how', are practical

'This year's Year 2 class has recently been working on the IPC My World unit. In groups, the children had to make a book about a country of their choice. One group chose Spain because they'd been on their class 'holiday' to Spain last year. Even one whole year on, they remembered all the details of that day 'flying' to Spain and their experiences when they arrived. It was fantastic to hear all their positive feelings about their time in Spain. They even accessed their Spanish 'holiday' pictures from My Pictures off the computer – all by themselves – and used them in a PowerPoint presentation to the rest of the class about their chosen country. Their knowledge and understanding of Spain is very good and I think it's because of the way they have learnt about it.

When we worked on the Places People Go unit we also learned about the history of holidays and how the options for holidays years ago were impacted by the less sophisticated transportation. We looked at how changes in transportation over the years have made a difference to the types of holidays we could enjoy here in England and also for people in Spain.'
(Vicky Sewell, Christ Church Church of England Primary School, Ellesmere Port, Cheshire)

Figure 9.9   Developing the holiday in Spain one year on

Figure 9.9 is a good example of the different ways young children can learn both knowledge and skills. It is also a good example of how engagement in the process of learning increases children's ability to remember what they have learned. The type of activities described here do take more time to set up and require more thinking from the teacher if they are to punch their 'learning' weight. But the pay-off is worth it. It is hard to believe that Year 2 children would have responded as they did one year on from the actual classroom learning experience if the teacher's careful execution had not allowed them an opportunity to fully engage and be engaged.

Interestingly, so much of what we mean by international-mindedness is 'caught' as well as 'taught'. In taking the time to carefully prepare the activities in this way, the teacher is both implicitly and explicitly demonstrating to the children in her own class the important values that will underpin the later development of a more mature international-mindedness.

Learning: subjects and their integration

This definition of learning is simply that; a definition of what happens when learning takes place. It has no values attached to it. Fagin taught Oliver and his fellow pickpockets so ably in Charles Dickens's *Oliver Twist* precisely because he had an intuitive sense of what learning was. Learning how to save the world and learning how to murder someone both use a remarkably similar method.

We begin to add values or a moral dimension to learning when we choose how to organize learning through our curriculum organization. Fagin chose his curriculum with very clear intentions in mind; we need to take the same care in schools, as every decision we take has implications for the successful learning children will hopefully achieve.

Recently, we have begun to revisit the debate about whether a curriculum should separate or integrate subjects. Learning can take place within both organizational methods. Both have strengths and weaknesses. Single-subject curriculums enable teachers and children to focus on the learning within subjects (Christiano Ronaldo), but they inhibit the opportunities for children to begin to see the links across subjects (Stephen Fry). Cross-curricular or integrated approaches can help children see the links between subjects but can fail to provide children with the opportunity to study any subject in depth.

It seems to us that we have to find a way to solve the problems inherent in cross-curricular teaching. Almost all of the personal issues our children will be facing in their lives, and almost all of the larger community and world issues they will be facing, require a multi-perspective and multidisciplinary approach. (It is impossible to think of solutions to the 'environment' that are only scientific or only geographical.) It is also the case that a cross-curricular approach that integrates more than one subject is more closely aligned with the way in which most people's brains are organized. It is an approach that is more congruent with the processes of learning.

Learning history and geography in the primary school

A significant part of our work over the past seven years has been the development of the International Primary Curriculum, now in use in schools in more than 50 countries including many schools in the UK.

We have designed this curriculum explicitly to provide children with cross-curricular approaches that can, at the same time, enable children to delve more deeply into each of the component subjects. Children's learning is organized around themes that appeal to them, while at the same time enabling rigorous learning objectives to be set. 'Chocolate' is a very good and, for some reason, popular example. Within that theme though, children learn science, history, geography, art and more, with each 'subject' being worked on continuously for a period of one or two weeks during the duration of the theme.

By choosing this method of organization we are helping children build their learning in individual subjects but also building up their networks of learning across subjects. We think that one of the reasons for the very positive response of teachers, parents and children to the IPC is because they recognize intuitively how it mirrors and supports the natural learning patterns of the brain.

According to the International Primary Curriculum, in history, children learn about the past in relation to the present (Skelton et al., 2004). At the same time, geography is the study of places. According to the IPC, in geography, children learn about places and environments in the world around them (Skelton et al., 2004).

What it means to develop international-mindedness in the primary school

There is general agreement that it is important for twenty-first-century children to become global citizens. Unfortunately, there is less agreement about what that means and at what stages of their development it is possible for children to become that. The resulting debate about these issues has produced any number of terms which mean something similar; 'global citizen' is just one of those. 'International citizens' is another such term, found helpful by many because it involves both 'inter' and 'national; immersion in one's own culture as well as the cultures of others.

What also happens is that terms like 'global citizenship' become a catch-all for many different kinds of undoubtedly worthwhile movements such as multiculturalism, peace studies, environmentalism and more. It is our view that while each of these contains the essence of global citizenship they are also much more than it. The question is, 'What is the essence of global citizenship?'

'Year 2 have been studying "Health" which has included learning about health centres where babies and children are immunised. This has led to a comparison of immunisations of children in other countries around the world. The children have been able to think about what it's like for other children in other countries who don't have the immunisation opportunities that we have here in the UK. They've been thinking of what it would be like to get smallpox and other diseases just because there isn't an immunisation programme.'
(Sheryl Wrigley, Deputy Head Teacher at St Aloysius Catholic Primary School in Huyton, Knowsley)

Figure 9.10   Health

We believe that at the heart of global citizenship or international-mindedness is an increasingly complex development of our relationship to the 'other'. Howard Gardner reverses this and calls the progress of human development 'a continual decline in egocentrism'. This is a helpful phrase as it makes it possible for us to compare a child going through the 'terrible twos' with Nelson Mandela's capacity for reconciliation with those who had imprisoned him and neglected many of his colleagues for so long. The child is full of egocentricity; Nelson Mandela has let it all go. Most of us do not seem able to ever reach that point.

The fact that so few of us manage to completely lose our egocentricity throughout our lives begins to suggest that it might be over-ambitious to hope that it can be achieved by children in the primary school. When children first come to school they are only just beginning the passage away from egocentricity. Parallel play, where children play alongside but not with other children, is one visible sign of the move; the first, real 'best friend' at around the age of 8 is another. The fact that children have only a few more primary school years to go suggests that the development of true global citizenship in the primary school is unlikely.

It is possible to 'fake' global citizenship in the primary school by getting children to express a kind of concern for those less fortunate than themselves. There is something admirable in this as a starting point, but the developmental capacities of primary-aged children and our lifetime of watching them at work and play suggest to us that we should come to accept that children's increasing appreciation for others who are different from them in and around their own home and cultural group should be seen as the 'Beginning' phase of global citizenship; one that primary schools can accept responsibility for and that children are capable of achieving. (It is not that some primary children will not transcend this stage but we cannot build a programme for all on targets that can be achieved only by the interpersonally gifted.)

The impact of history and geography on international-mindedness

History and geography both have a significant contribution to make to the early development of our appreciation of the other. Stories about people who lived in or around the neighbourhood help young children begin to get a sense not only of 'now' and 'then' but also that life was different than their life is today. Asking children to think why certain actions were taken in history or why certain events happened helps children to come to see that there are different possible answers and that even their own friends can hold views different from their own. Enabling children to look at primary source material enables them to see that judgements have to be made based on and supported by the best evidence that is available. Each of these skills will be vital when children develop a greater and broader awareness of the other and begin to be able to explore outside their own culture or locality.

Similarly, learning about the changes in a local environment helps children see that things are rarely the same, even in their own locality; difference becomes as normal as similarity. Engagement in environmental improvement projects brings children face to face with a multiplicity of perspectives and attitudes towards what is acceptable. Moving out of one's immediate locality to other different localities on fieldwork helps children to familiarize themselves with the fact that different lives to theirs are led by others nearby.

Each of these experiences, and the many others offered by history, geography and other subjects in school, is crucial in helping children to develop a sense of the other, provided we take advantage of them in this way. Each helps children to make a particular series of connections in their brain that hopefully becomes consolidated enough to impact on how children think of cultures and world issues that are significantly different from their own.

But we should not delude ourselves that this impact is a given. It is possible for everything to have both a benefit and a pathology; a positive and a negative contribution. It is not history or geography per se that contribute to the development of global citizenship; it is our ability to work with the material offered to us by history and geography that contributes to the creation of global citizenship. A history based only on national glorification will build up a network of consolidated neurons that cannot interpret anything other than through a simplistic single filter; a geography based only on an unchanging view of landscape, environment, community and trade will do the same.

In the same way that global citizenship involves an appreciation of both one's own nation and culture and the nations and cultures of others, so one's personal development involves both the self and the other. Providing we choose to use opportunity to develop both, history and

IPC unit, Up, Up and Away

geography have an important part to play in the development of twenty-first-century citizens.

In the case studies used in this chapter there is a development of understanding of history and geography. It is quite apparent that these children are beginning to recognize that history and geography are more than learning facts and how to do certain things; that history and geography involve learning an integral part of who we are, our identity and ways in which we are the same as and different from others. Through this understanding, the move from 'self' to 'other' – in other words, a developing international-mindedness – is possible for primary-age children.

References

Gardner, H. (2008) *Five Minds for the Future*. Boston, MA: Harvard Business School Press.

Skelton, M. et al. (2004) *The International Primary Curriculum*. London: Fieldwork Education.

10

Using dialogue to engage children with challenging ideas: geography and global citizenship

Donna Hurford

Chapter introduction

This chapter explores how two Year 6 (Y6) classes, from two primary schools in the same town in north-west England, engaged with aspects of social justice, a global citizenship concept identified in Oxfam (2006) and Department for International Development and Department for Education and Skills (DfID/DfES, 2005), through an enquiry-based approach based on Philosophy for Children (P4C), WL 10.3 (www.sapere.org.uk). The main aim of the project was to explore how the Year 6 children engaged with ethical issues associated with community linking, such as their understanding of partnership and the implications of trade and aid.

The project provides opportunities to review and critique the cross-curricular potential of an integrated global citizenship and P4C approach and to discuss how we can assess the effects on children's learning and engagement with ethical issues.

As stimuli provide the thought-provoking focus for enquiries, the children were introduced to a wide range including: a Peters Projection world map; a globe; factual information about food distribution; artefacts from specific African countries; a Malawian story about creativity and partnership with accompanying photographs

(Continued)

(Continued)

and wire toys; a fictional story, created by the facilitator, about creativity and charity; a role play about charity and partnership, created
and enacted by the facilitator; photographs and hand-drawn maps of
a Ghanaian village community.

Analysis of the recordings indicates that many children engaged
with challenging social justice issues through sessions that were
cross-curricular in nature, addressing aspects of a range of subjects
including: geography, design and technology, citizenship, PSHE and
literacy.

The project also revealed some dilemmas. When P4C is context
based, in this case to focus attention on global citizenship issues, it may
be used as a learning tool rather than an approach to teaching and
learning. Open Spaces for Dialogue and Enquiry (OSDE) offers an alternative dialogic approach to engaging with global issues and interdependence. While P4C's focus on the development of high-order
philosophical thinking, careful listening and dialogue can encourage
creative and participatory engagement, some learners, for example
those who struggle to articulate their thoughts, may be excluded
from some of the process.

Aims of the project

1 Explore how Year 6 children at a primary school in north-west England
  engaged with the concept of social justice, through a cross-curricular
  approach, with a particular focus on the ethical issues associated with
  their local community's partnership with a village community in Ghana.
2 Evaluate the effectiveness and appropriateness of Philosophy for
  Children as a way to engage the children in dialogue and enquiry
  about the ethical issues.

Developing the project: cross-curricular approaches

Figure 10.1 presents a visual interpretation of the key concepts, skills, values
and attitudes that were addressed through the project. The list of developing behaviours, on the right-hand side, indicates how the children
demonstrated their learning as the project developed. When planning the
project it was evident that the pupils and the facilitator would be involved
with a multilayered, integrated approach to learning. This approach would
explore concepts including social justice and partnership, develop skills

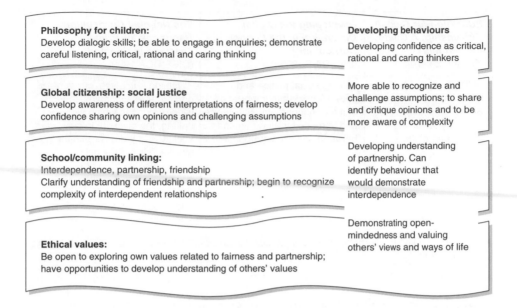

Figure 10.1 Concepts, skills, values and attitudes addressed through the Year 6 P4C/GC project

including dialogue and types of thinking, and challenge values and attitudes. The horizontal lines in Figure 10.1 are deliberately wavy to represent the potential for integrated learning across the four strands.

Unlike current accepted practice, specific learning objectives were not identified by the facilitator or shared with the children. The integrated plan provided a flexible framework, which was 'open to unanticipated outcomes' (Steiner, 1993: 26). Time was given, at the end of each session, for personal and paired reflection on what had been learnt or how thinking about issues had changed. This approach to planning and assessment was based on the principles of Assessment for Learning (Assessment Reform Group, 2002) and provided opportunities to assess children's engagement through their verbal contributions and their non-verbal behaviour or their level of 'flow' (Csikszentmihayli, cited in Barnes, 2007: 228). Barnes (2007: 229) and Fisher (2000: 65) discuss how noticing children's physical behaviour can provide insights into their level of engagement with learning; as the project's P4C sessions progressed, the children's behaviour suggested that they were listening attentively, reflecting on their peers' comments and planning their own examples of contributions.

Despite the current, 2008, non-statutory status of both citizenship and global citizenship in the primary National Curriculum for England, the global citizenship concepts identified in DfES/DfID (2005) and Oxfam (2006) offer thematic opportunities for cross-curricular learning that could enable pupils to meaningfully engage with the values that underpin the National Curriculum, as illustrated in Figure 10.2.

Education for Global Citizenship: A Guide for Schools (Oxfam, 2006)	Developing the Global Dimension in the School Curriculum (DfID/DfES, 2005)	The National Curriculum: Handbook for Primary Teachers in England (DfEE/QCA,1999)
Willingness to speak up for others; Sense of justice; Empathy for others locally and globally. (2006: 4)	Valuing social justice and understanding the importance of it for ensuring equality, justice and fairness for all within and between societies. (2005: 8–9)	...valuing ourselves, our families and other relationships, the wider groups to which we belong, the diversity in our society and the environment in which we live. Education should also reaffirm our commitment to the virtues of truth, justice, honesty, trust and a sense of duty. (1999: 10)

Figure 10.2 Global citizenship concepts identified in DfEE/QCA (1999), DfID/DfES (2005), and Oxfam (2006)

Developing understanding of social justice through National Curriculum values

According to Dahlberg and Moss, 'The task of ethics is to formulate higher principles or criteria within a society' (2005: 66). It could, therefore, be argued that an education system that is based on 'truth, justice, honesty, trust and a sense of duty' (DfES/QCA, 1999 p.10) would both want and need its educators and learners to develop their understanding of society's ethical values. Evidence of the English education system's commitment to social justice can be found in the non-statutory guidance for Key Stage 2 citizenship: 'They (pupils) develop their sense of social justice and moral responsibility and begin to understand that their own choices and behaviour can affect local, national or global issues and political and social institutions' (DfES/QCA, 1999: 139).

Developing understanding of social justice through values associated with philosophy for children

In order to engage with a society's ethics, Dahlberg and Moss argue that we need some essential qualities: 'reason, abstraction and impartiality' (2005: 66). In addition, the learner needs to be able to philosophically engage with controversial issues. Philosophy for children offers an enquiry approach to learning (see Figure 10.3 and Society for the Advancement of Philosophical Enquiry and Reflection in Education (SAPERE) for more information on P4C) through which a range of skills are learnt and applied. These skills include rational, logical and caring thinking and dialogic skills. As these skills develop, participants can become better equipped and more confident about questioning assumptions and challenging misconceptions and prejudices. According to Lipman et al., teaching children how to think for themselves can offer them a philosophical approach to lifelong learning as it, 'requires appraisal of one's own values and in effect of one's own

P4C enquiry process adopted through the project	Comments on how this process worked in practice
Develop the community of trust by reviewing the core rules: respectful listening; share your own opinion when you are ready; agree or disagree with a peer's contribution; be prepared for someone to question you or challenge your opinion, look for evidence for opinions.	The children responded positively to the rules and over the two terms became more familiar with the conventions for contributions to an enquiry, such as 'I agree with A because … ' or 'I disagree with A because … .'
Start with co-operative games that the children were invited to deconstruct.	The games featured highly in the children's feedback, 'fun and interesting, never played them before' (Year 6, July 2008); favourites were often requested. Provided a practical way to develop all of the children's collaborative skills.
Children and facilitator sit in a circle	Reinforced equal status and facilitated eye-contact. Even children who did not contribute to the dialogues were participants in the enquiry process.
Facilitator shares a stimulus for the enquiry.	A variety of stimuli were used including: Peter's Projection world map; globe; factual information about food distribution; artefacts from specific African countries; a Malawian story about creativity and partnership with accompanying photos and wire toys; a fictional story, created by the facilitator, about creativity and charity; a role play about charity and partnership, created and enacted by the facilitator, photographs and hand-drawn maps of the Ghanaian village community.
Children have time to reflect individually on the stimulus followed by group work, composing questions that could engage all participants in a discussion where there could be different opinions and challenging thinking.	The opening games were often used to regroup children. Feedback from the children included 'liked group work, sharing ideas'. The facilitator circulated around the groups listening to questions being developed and encouraging the groups to reflect on whether the questions would provide opportunities for deep thinking and different opinions.
Each group writes its question on the flip-chart sheet.	Led to groups refining their questions and having a sense of ownership. Sometimes the strength of the feeling of ownership affected the children's impartiality when voting.
Each participant votes for the question that they think will lead to the most interesting enquiry.	The children were encouraged to close their eyes if they thought they would be influenced by their peers' choices.

(Continued)

Figure 10.3 . *(Continued)*

P4C enquiry process adopted through the project	Comments on how this process worked in practice
The question with the most votes is selected	The voting process varied, sometimes one or two votes each, but the majority vote always secured the question for the enquiry.
The facilitator facilitates rather than contributes to the discussions	The facilitator tried to limit her contributions to modelling Socratic questioning; encouraging the children to clarify their comments, provide evidence for opinions and to consider alternative views. As the children became more familiar with the process many of the children's contributions indicated more careful listening, and they adopted some of the models shared by the facilitator

Figure 10.3   The Philosophy for Children enquiry process evaluated in this example

identity ... a search for more and more reliable criteria so that the judgements one makes in the course of one's life can rest upon a firm and solid foundation' (1980: 203).

To support and encourage the Year 6 children's engagement with ethical issues about social justice, and in the later enquiries more specifically on aspects of community linking, the children were given time to think for themselves and were guided on how to construct and deconstruct their understanding by listening and sharing their opinions through respectful dialogue. Although the UK school was not directly linked with a school in the Ghanaian village there was evidence of the community link, including a strong local commitment to Fair Trade and exchange visits by members of both communities. As the focus of this project was on exploring children's engagement with the ethical issues associated with this community partnership it was seen as especially important to provide opportunities for critical, creative and caring thinking. Caring thinking is identified by Lipman as a philosophical approach to thinking about ethical issues (Lipman, 1991, cited in Haynes, 2002: 37) and explained by Haynes (2002: 40) as an approach that can help us understand our behaviours towards others and the nature of our emotional engagement.

Developing understanding of social justice through values associated with global citizenship

The DfES/DfID's (2005) focus on social justice identifies opportunities to develop learners' knowledge and understanding by 'understanding the importance of it (social justice) for ensuring equality, justice and fairness for all within and between societies'; develop learners' skills by 'challenging racism and other forms of discrimination' and develop learners' values by 'valuing social justice' (2005: 8–9). In comparison, Oxfam's (2006) model provides an arguably more coherent framework for progressive learning about GC, by explicitly integrating elements of knowledge and understanding, skills and values and attitudes. According to Oxfam (2006) learners can develop their knowledge and understanding about 'social justice and equity' (2006: 4) and engage with values and attitudes by learning and applying relevant skills. These skills include thinking critically, arguing effectively, challenging injustice and inequalities, respecting people and co-operating. The Oxfam (2006) model could be interpreted as an approach to teaching and learning rather than a set of knowledge-based concepts. A view shared by Young and Commins, 'At Oxfam Education we believe Global Citizenship is more than the sum of its parts' (2002: 1).

Developing understanding of social justice through values associated with philosophy for children and global citizenship

Therefore, both P4C and global citizenship offer approaches to teaching and learning that focus on participation and a readiness to challenge assumptions and perceived knowledge. Hicks's (2007: 25) adaptation of Pike and Selby's model of global citizenship includes a 'process dimension' 'that requires a holistic and participatory approach that focuses on exploration of differing values perspectives and which leads to politically aware local and global citizenship' (Hicks, 2007: 25). However, what evidence is there that young learners want to engage with values-based education and why would this engagement necessarily lead to political awareness? If we regard learner motivation as an intrinsic part of effective learning, then involving children in identifying a topic for further study could encourage ownership and commitment to the project. One of the Year 6 class teachers involved with the project commented on how surprised she was that the quieter, less confident children in the class were willing to express their opinions about social justice issues.

Fisher quotes a child's comment on people's relationship with the environment: 'We know so much about the world but we don't always do what's good for the world' (1998: 293). This illustrates Lipman et al.'s argument for enabling children to develop their thinking about ethical issues 'they (children) want to know what matters and what does not matter' (1980: 39). One of the tenets of global citizenship (GC) is that children must not feel disempowered and overwhelmed by global issues. The Primary Review's *Community Soundings* acknowledges how primary schools that engaged learners with local and global issues led to the children feeling more positive about their contribution: 'we can do something about it' (Primary Review, 2007: 16). Giving children the opportunity to reflect on challenging issues, to share their opinions while engaging with others' views, can provide young learners with meaningful opportunities to make sense of the world. A thematic, integrated approach to learning as advocated by Barnes (2007) can incorporate challenging issues while providing explicit or implicit links with areas of knowledge, skills development and engagement with values and attitudes. If we believe that effective learning starts with the learner, Barnes's notion of a 'curriculum for hope' (2007: 126) based on Frierean ideals becomes a possibility.

Planning the P4C enquiries

The Year 6 classes, involved with the project, had no prior experience of P4C and the sessions were planned and facilitated by a university tutor with a strong interest in both global citizenship and P4C and with some P4C training. A significant critique of the project is how the focus for the P4C enquiries was selected, as the facilitator specifically sought schools with a link with a community in the South (as a generic term for lesser economically developed countries), with the intention of exploring how children engaged with the associated ethical issues. Although this proposed focus was discussed with the teachers involved and had their agreement, it was not a topic that was identified by the children. The children responded positively to the sessions but it would have been interesting and more congruent with Assessment for Learning if the children had been involved in identifying a topic for enquiry. However, the P4C process does include autonomous decision-making by the participants with regard to selecting the questions for the enquiries, giving the children the opportunity to demonstrate choosing in each enquiry. The facilitator initially offered to run six fortnightly enquiries, each lasting between 40 and 60 minutes at each school; the enquiries continued with one of the schools for a further six sessions. First, the P4C process was explained to the children and they were introduced to the core rules for enquiry sessions. See Figure 10.3 for an outline of the P4C enquiry process as applied through the project and related comments.

Nature of the stimuli used in the enquiries

As the children had no prior experience of P4C and, as far as the facilitator was aware, they had not engaged in sustained learning about their community link with the Ghanaian village, the stimuli provided opportunities to focus on significant concepts associated with community linking and partnership. Having only limited time for each enquiry, often less than 30 minutes, the stimuli had to be engaging and easily accessible to the children so a range of visual, auditory and tangible resources was used. Although the facilitator had some stimuli in mind at the start of the project, she preferred to be informed by the children's learning and their engagement with each enquiry. After each enquiry the facilitator reflected on the areas of the children's thinking that revealed significant assumptions and stereotypes, and selected stimuli that could invite further discussion about those issues.

Throughout all the enquiries the children engaged with aspects of social justice; however, the choice of stimulus provided the opportunity for a more specific focus. The stimuli for the initial enquiry were selected to gauge children's awareness and responsiveness to inequitable food distribution and drew on information from a non-fiction book for children, *If the World Were a Village* (Smith, 2004), and a variety of real lunch boxes each containing foods with different nutritional content. Contributions to this enquiry revealed both a commitment to food redistribution but also a sense of paternalism with a focus on giving to the poor. In an attempt to challenge this perception of people in the south being dependent and needy, in the next enquiry examples of Malawian children's creativity and resourcefulness, such as home-made wire toys, were used as stimuli. Creativity and resourcefulness were recurrent themes and featured strongly in the story used for the last enquiry.

The facilitator identified a need to help the children engage with the concept of partnership and linking, and in the next enquiry they were given the opportunity to reflect and clarify their own perceptions of friendship, starting with an adaptation of the activity 'Relationship strings' as a stimulus. Before focusing on the community link, some sessions were used to develop the children's background knowledge of the Ghanaian village and the significance of Fair Trade. The concept of community linking and partnership was relatively unfamiliar to the children, and the facilitator designed and enacted a short role play that included two characters, demonstrating different approaches to supporting a family in the Ghanaian village. The last enquiry included a story about charity and valuing creativity and interdependence. It was created and told by the facilitator, and was accompanied by examples of creative and resourceful artefacts from South Africa. The benefits of using bespoke and varied stimuli were evident: the children's curiosity was aroused and they were motivated to engage in thought-provoking discussions.

The following section includes evaluative accounts of the children's learning and engagement through five representative enquiries:

1 Global food distribution. Stimuli: non-fiction text and lunch boxes.
2 Creativity and resourcefulness. Stimuli: Malawian children's story, photographs and wire toys.
3 Friendship. Stimulus: 'Friendship strings' activity.
4 Partnership and interdependence. Stimulus: role play.
5 Partnership and interdependence. Stimulus: story with accompanying artefacts.

Enquiry 1: Global food distribution

Stimuli: Non-fiction text and lunch boxes.
Emerging themes: social justice, fairness, charity, perceptions of others.

Having checked with the class teacher that no children in the class were known to be at risk or to have eating disorders and might be disturbed by the focus on food and poverty, global food distribution was selected as the initial stimulus. Using information from Smith (2004), and a selection of three lunch boxes containing foods that represented a starvation diet, minimum subsistence and a more than sufficient diet, the children were encouraged to frame possible questions that the whole class could discuss. The children worked in four groups and each group composed a question that was offered to the whole class. Each child was then asked to vote for one question from the list, see below, that they thought would stimulate the most interesting discussion.

1 Why did the 20 people not get enough money?
2 Why can't they just share?
3 Do we really need this much food?
4 Why do the 30 per cent have more than the other 70 per cent?

Question 2 was selected by the majority, although in this enquiry, as all of the questions focused on fairness, the children also engaged with aspects of the other questions. This enquiry provided opportunities for the children to engage with a variety of concepts, skills, values and attitudes through a cross-curricular approach (see Figure 10.4).

Challenging stereotypes
This enquiry provoked strong opinions about fairness and some children found the notion of unequal food distribution incomprehensible, as

Enquiry 1 : Global food distribution		
Concepts: knowledge and understanding	**Skills**	**Values and attitudes**
Geog: sense of place, food distribution **Maths:** world population represented as a village model, percentages **DT/ECM:** healthy eating **Language:** knowing appropriate language – I agree because … , I disagree because … **RE/PSHE:** awareness of others, fairness **Citizenship:** voting systems, own rights and responsibilities **Global Citizenship:** social justice, interdependence and globalisation, human rights and responsibilities	Co-operation Analysing stimulus Framing questions Evaluating questions Logical, creative, caring thinking Voting Speaking and listening Assume appropriate role in group Turn-taking Sharing opinions Responding Challenging opinions Developing arguments Reflect on own learning	Co-operative Supportive Sense of self … I think Patience Giving constructive feedback … Respect for others' views Acceptance of different opinions Open-mindedness Mindfulness of others Empathy

Figure 10.4 Concepts, skills, values and attitudes in the enquiry

illustrated in the chosen question, 'Why can't they just share?' They suggested a range of actions for the world community, predominantly based on sending food from wealthy countries to poor countries. The children did not tend to share opinions about why some countries had more food than others, although in later enquiries some children commented on people's willingness to work hard and the effects of climate. A P4C enquiry using the same stimulus was also used with the Year 6 class in the neighbouring school, however, there were twins in this class who had lived, for some time, in an African country. The twins drew on their own personal experiences and their comments indicated an awareness and understanding of the issues associated with poverty and injustice; they often challenged their peers' stereotypes and opinions that were assumption rather than evidence based. This illustrates an opportunity in a global citizenship/P4C session to identify children's lack of knowledge or misconceptions in a complementary subject area, in this case looking at geographical and historical reasons for poverty, providing a meaningful cross-curricular link with a future lesson.

Contributing to the enquiry

In the initial enquiries the children tended to share their individual opinions more than respond to others' contributions. This preference was evident at the start of all enquiries: it was as if all their concentration was needed to remember their own points, preventing them from engaging with the listening process. This compelling need for some children to make their own contribution to the discussion could be assessed as evidence of engagement and 'flow' (Csikszentmihayli, cited in Barnes, 2007: 228), however, the contributions tended to be very similar and once the children had listened and responded using the starters 'I agree' or 'I disagree', the dialogue indicated more reflective thinking. The facilitator occasionally reminded them about listening to others and responding to points, and to make this more conscious a signalling system was adopted: a raised arm for a response, an arm stretched out in front to make a new point and tapping the head with both hands if the desire to speak was all consuming. The signals also made it clear to the others who wanted to speak and after a few enquiries the children responded to the signals and decided who would speak next; passing ownership to the community and away from the facilitator.

Enquiry 2: Creativity and resourcefulness

Stimuli: Malawian children's story, photographs and wire toys.
Emerging themes: Imagination, creativity, challenging stereotypes, universal ethical questions.

Having reflected on the initial enquiries it was evident that the children were engaging with aspects of social justice and demonstrating their beliefs in different approaches to wealth redistribution as possible solutions. However, their engagement with the issues tended to be objective, which was to be expected, having presented them with a global social justice stimulus. There was also a tendency to advocate paternalistic approaches, for example, from people in the UK need to look after poor people in Africa, to tackling poverty without an awareness of people's resourcefulness and rights to identify their own needs. In an attempt to personalize the links with children from a community in the south and to see how the children would respond to examples of other children's creativity, resources from the DT pack *Toying with Technology* (Brand, 2000) were provided as stimuli. These stimuli included a picture-book story about a boy in Malawi who makes his own wire toy, known as a Galimoto, with accompanying photographs of Malawian children making and playing with wire toys, examples of real wire toys and a world map. Before starting the enquiry, the children found Malawi on the world map and were reminded that the story was about children living in a village in Malawi, in an attempt to clarify confusion and assumptions about Africa being a continent and not a country.

Comments on creativity

The Year 6 children were very interested in the wire toys. They were impressed by the Malawian children's skills and resourcefulness, and intrigued by their ability to fashion models using unsophisticated tools and recycled materials. Some commented on how they would not know how to make a Galimoto and that children in the UK are more likely to play with an X-Box than to make their own toys. A previous enquiry that focused on play led to thoughts on imagination and creativity, including 'Can have it (imagination) anywhere, always with them/us' and a thought-provoking question,' 'Does everyone have an imagination?' The question they chose for this creativity enquiry indicated an interest in how different toys compared as sources of fun:

> Are the toys, the children in the story play with, as much fun as ours? (Year 6, November, 2007)

Unanticipated opportunities for engagement

Although the stimulus was chosen as a way to engage the children with other children's creativity and resourcefulness, the story includes ethical issues such as possible theft and sibling jealousy, which tended to be the focus of the enquiries with both Year 6 classes. As the participants' ownership of the enquiry question is a critical part of P4C enquiries, the facilitator has to be open and receptive to the enquiry community's areas of interest. The focus on the potential theft and the fraternal relationship provided an unanticipated opportunity (Steiner, 1993) to further develop rapport as the Year 6 children were able to make personal connections through universally relevant questions: Is it ever right to steal? How do you cope with sibling jealousy? Some of the contributions to the enquiry included awareness of the complexity of reasons for sibling jealousy:

> If the older brother had tried to make one and someone older than him could have said that he couldn't have made one, he would feel quite sad but keep trying to do it.

> I agree with E because the older brother thought, I'm the oldest so I have to be the coolest, can't let my brother beat me. (Year 6 children, November 2007)

However, this does highlight a possible tension when contextualizing P4C, although the facilitator may choose a stimulus with a specific focus in mind there is no guarantee that the children will be attracted to the implicit or even explicit focus. Weblink 10.2 Open Spaces for Dialogue and Enquiry's (OSDE) (www.osdemethodology. org.uk) explicit focus on global issues, perspectives and interdependence may offer a more congruent dialogic approach. Nevertheless, having the opportunity to see the photographs and handle the wire toys provided tangible experiences for the children that did help them refocus on notions of creativity and resourcefulness.

Comments indicating values

When asked at the end of the enquiry what it had made them think about, most responses from one Year 6 class focused on the types of toys children have in Africa, with some comments indicating reflections on valuing what they have and social responsibilities:

> Children in Africa, what they play with and how we can help them ... how African children can make Galimotos ... how lucky we are to have toys and houses to live in. (Year 6 children, December 2007)

The tendency to use Africa as a generic name for all African countries was still evident and indicated a need for further work on map skills. Although the children had demonstrated that they valued the Malawian children's creativity, their concluding comments indicated that they attributed a higher value to their own homes and toys, and they became more aware of what they perceived to be their own good fortune. As discussed by Disney (2003) further enquiries on perceptions of wealth could help children challenge these assumptions and engage more deeply with values associated with global citizenship. Figure 10.5 provides an overview of the cross-curricular learning that was highlighted in the creativity enquiries together with opportunities to further develop the thematic approach. The Year 6 children asked if we could make Galimotos. Designing and making their own wire toys would have provided a relevant (Barnes, 2007: 187) learning opportunity for the children to discover their own creative resourcefulness.

Enquiry 3: Friendship

> Stimulus: 'Friendship strings' activity.
> Emerging themes: Acceptance of imperfection, unconditionality, shared values, valuing communication, deepening friendship.

Defining the concept of friendship provided the children with opportunities to clarify their thinking and to engage with the possibility that friendship may include inconsistent behaviour. The opening game for this enquiry was an adaptation of 'Relationship strings', renamed 'Friendship

Enquiry 2: Creativity and resourcefulness		
Concepts: knowledge and understanding	Skills	Values and attitudes
Geog: map skills, recognizing a continent and a country **DT:** design, using recycled materials, selecting tools, evaluating product, creativity **Language:** knowing appropriate language – I agree because … , I disagree because … **RE/PSHE:** recognizing talents and skills, understanding jealousy, stealing: is it ever right? **Citizenship:** responsibilities **Global Citizenship:** social justice, interdependence and globalization, human rights and responsibilities	Co-operation Analysing stimulus Framing questions Evaluating questions Logical, creative, caring thinking Voting Speaking and listening Assume appropriate role in group Turn-taking Sharing opinions Responding Challenging opinions Developing arguments Reflect on own learning	Co-operative Supportive Sense of self … I think Patience Giving constructive feedback … Respect for other's views Acceptance of different opinions Open-mindedness Mindfulness of others Empathy Showing understanding Celebrating creativity Curiosity

Figure 10.5 An overview of the cross-curricular learning

strings'. The children stood in a circle and passed around a ball of string, giving a reason why the child they were passing it to was their friend. Each receiver of the string kept hold of it and, as it can be received more than once by any player, the string formed a web. Once all of the string was used, the children were asked to keep it taut and to reflect on what it represented and to consider the effects if one or more let go. When deconstructing the game the children recognized the interconnectedness of their friendships, as visualized by the web, and the effects on the class if friendships broke down. The game also formed the stimulus for the enquiry and the children chose the question 'Why do friends make people happy?' (Year 6, January 2008). Initially the children's contributions to the enquiry expressed high expectations and exclusively positive perceptions of friendship:

> A true friend will always be there for you and never make you upset;
> Always there for you when you are hurt;
> Funny, helpful, don't leave you out;
> Always stick by you and never make you feel upset;
> Someone who helps you, likes you and never lies to you. (Year 6, January 2008)

What is also evident is that the children framed their contributions as how they wanted a friend to treat them; although reciprocity may be inferred it was not explicitly expressed. One child's contribution, that revealed an acceptance of imperfection, provided the stimulus for more critical thinking about friendship:

> A friend is someone who cares for you but friends can't always be perfect. (Year 6, January 2008)

Although some of the children had already demonstrated that they could engage with complexity and there was evidence of some recognition that values are not necessarily absolute and universally shared, this was a significant comment for the effect it had on the others' thinking. Children began to reflect more on the reality of friendship rather than their ideals; they identified reasons for less than perfect behaviour and acknowledged that falling out with a friend may benefit the relationship. A child, who demonstrated some aspects of behaviour associated with the autistic spectrum, shared a logical rationale for a friend not being able to offer support:

> If you were in need, might not always be there for you because sometimes might be away and not able to stick by you. (Year 6, January 2008)

Others in the group shared their opinions on the value of being able to argue with a friend and the belief in friendship's unconditionality:

> If you argue with a friend that's what makes them an actual friend because could be good, could be the start of a friendship and then start talking more.

> OK, if you argue with a friend or fall out because that's like a common friendship and you'll get back together sooner or later. (Year 6, January 2008)

The notion of arguing being a catalyst for more communicative friendship suggests an awareness of the complexity of communication and the risk-taking that may be necessary to open up discussions. The comment also indicates that challenges and differences in a friendship are valued as they provide opportunities to deepen the friendship, which echoes aims for diversity education, to value similarities and differences (Oxfam, 2006). The same child who contributed the comment on a friend being less than perfect went on to say 'arguing can make you more confident in talking in front of your friends', suggesting a link being made between being able to 'argue effectively' (Oxfam 2006, p. 4) and developing 'a sense of identify and self esteem' (ibid.). This enquiry revealed a depth of critical and caring thinking about friendship, stimulated by one child's comment on the acceptance of imperfection, giving the facilitator the opportunity to encourage further reflection on their definitions of friendship. Figure 10.6 provides a possible interpretation of the actual and potential cross-curricular learning inspired by the friendship enquiry.

Enquiry 3: Friendship		
Concepts: knowledge and understanding	Skills	Values and attitudes
DT: design and evaluate a structure: web making **Language:** knowing appropriate language – I agree because … , I disagree because … **RE/PSHE:** awareness of self, and others, expectations of friendship **Citizenship:** roles and responsibilities **Global Citizenship:** self-concept, diversity, interdependence	Co-operation Analysing stimulus Framing questions Evaluating questions Critical, caring thinking Voting Speaking and listening Assume appropriate role in group Turn-taking Sharing opinions Responding Challenging opinions Developing arguments Reflect on own learning	Co-operative Supportive Value self and others Sense of self … I think Patience Giving constructive feedback … Respect for others' views Acceptance of different opinions Open-mindedness Mindfulness of others Empathy Showing understanding Celebrating diversity Curiosity

Figure 10.6 An interpretation of the actual and potential cross-curricular learning inspired by the friendship enquiry

Introduction to local community link with Ghanaian village

Awareness of ICT as a communication tool

Before embarking on an enquiry on partnership, time was given to identifying what the children knew about the link with the community in Ghana and their understanding of Fair Trade. As it was clear that the children had only some awareness of their community link, more time was given to exploring information in the form of photographs and hand-drawn maps, about the Ghanaian community. The children shared their fascination with the maps and photos and sought to make sense of what appeared to be a very different way of life. One session reviewing these resources and photographs of children from diverse communities led to a discussion about ways in which we can maintain long-distance friendships. Many of the children had holidayed abroad and made friends with other children, mainly from the UK, with whom they stayed in touch using web-based technologies like email, Skype, chat rooms as well as texts and phone calls. One child, who up to that point had tended not to contribute to enquiries, enthusiastically shared her knowledge about web-based translation programmes used by her sister to stay in touch with a foreign penfriend. Although UK classrooms provide primary-age children with opportunities to demonstrate and learn a wide range of ICT skills, it was revelatory to hear the children share their knowledge about technological communication, with such confidence and awareness, and suggested a potential topic on communication that could include aspects of language, ICT, DT, MFL, geography, history and citizenship/PSHE.

Using images as stimuli

Having looked at the resources on the Ghanaian community, the children were asked to consider what questions would be popular if they could have a P4C session with children from the link community; resulting in a vote for the question 'What are the differences and similarities between G (UK community) and K (Ghanaian community)?' (Year 6, March 2008).

The enquiry included reflections on social justice and food re-emerged as a theme: 'We are selfish in Britain because we waste a lot of food, families in the Ghanaian village would not be so wasteful' (Year 6, March 2008). This opinion was supported by another child who shared news he had remembered from a television programme that for every ten plates of food in the UK we waste seven. This evidence of interest in attitudes to food would have provided a relevant cross-curricular learning opportunity that could have included aspects of geography, DT, literacy and citizenship/global citizenship.

The photographs of life in the Ghanaian village provided realistic snapshots of village life, with adults and children working and playing as well as just posing for photographs. There were no images of mal-nourished, desperate people as the community has been able to provide for all village members because of the successful production of cocoa beans, some of which are traded through the Fair Trade organization. Nevertheless, the photographs do show the homes, buildings and roads to be less substantial structures than those in the UK and the village children are often wearing ill-fitting clothes and most are not wearing shoes, images that were interpreted by the children as evidence of economic poverty. As many media images of African and other developing countries often focus on situations of extreme poverty and destitution, it is understandable that these form points of reference for children when interpreting alternative images of community life.

Images can provide particularly powerful stimuli that viewers, including children, interpret by drawing on their prior knowledge. As viewers try to assimilate an image of a previously unfamiliar situation into their schema, the interpretation process will also be affected by their own values and attitudes; which suggests that allowing additional time for open and honest discussions about values and perceptions would be beneficial. When teaching about global citizenship, teachers have a responsibility to ensure children have the skills and awareness to challenge stereotypes and assumptions. Children also need guidance on how to develop their awareness of how absolute poverty can be addressed and to engage with different perceptions of wealth and poverty.

Some comments by the Year 6 children indicated that they were grappling with a contradiction; while the photos provided evidence of material poverty, the people looked happy and appeared to be having fun. This dilemma was highlighted in one of the questions suggested for the creativity enquiry: 'Why do the people in the pictures always seem to be happy even when they don't have as much as other people?' (Year 6, December 2007). Contradictions and dilemmas became more apparent in the last two enquiries that focused particularly on partnership between people from a UK locality like theirs and with people in a village community similar to that of the Ghanaian village.

Enquiry 4: Partnership and Interdependence

Stimulus 4: Role play.
Emerging themes: pragmatic, logical and caring thinking, aware of the consequences of action or inaction, predict outcomes, challenging stereotypes, seeking evidence.

Up to this point the stimuli chosen for the enquiries were mainly visual and kinaesthetic, with the use of a story for the creativity enquiry. Experienced P4C facilitators often recommend the use of specially written philosophical stories such as 'Kio and Gus' (Lipman and Sharp, 1986) because they focus on philosophical dilemmas and provide supportive frameworks for both the participants and the less experienced facilitator. Use of these texts is also more likely to preserve the integrity of the philosophical nature of the enquiry as there are fewer distractions for the listeners and thinkers. However, as the enquiries had shown evidence of the children's developmental engagement with the enquiry process and in order to maintain the focus on ethical issues associated with community linking, a bespoke role play and story were used for the last two enquiries.

The role play, devised and enacted by the facilitator, showed two Western visitors to a family in the Ghanaian village: the family was represented by a photograph of a family in the village, all of whom were very smartly dressed and stood in front of a car and a house. The first visitor was very benevolent and at times paternalistic; she came laden with gifts including food, radio, MP3 player and toys and said she would bring more but gave no indication that she wanted to have a discussion with the family or develop a friendship or partnership. By contrast the second visitor brought no material gifts, was much quieter and more reflective and asked if they would be interested in developing a partnership to find out more about each others' lives and see what they could learn from each other and how they could support each other.

Responses to the stimuli

The children demonstrated significant engagement with the role play; they listened and watched and were able to suspend disbelief despite both roles being played by the facilitator. In response to the role play they chose the question 'Which person would help the most and why?' (Year 6, March 2008). The question provided opportunities for assumptions and stereotypes to be revealed and challenged and for examples of deep, critical, creative and caring thinking to be demonstrated. Assumptions on the worth of bringing tinned food were countered by a child asking for evidence:

> A: Like the food, they would not have anything to cook it on.
> B: I disagree with A because we don't know they haven't got anything to cook it on ... (Year 6, March 2008)

Donating the MP3 player provoked significant interest and led to a discussion about the universality of the English language. The exchange quoted below reveals stereotypical views and how some children were drawing on prior knowledge to challenge these assumptions:

> S: No point having an MP3 player because probably never heard of English music before ... won't know how to switch it on because they never saw what an MP3 player looks like.
> E: Might not know because they are not as well educated as we are in this country.
> J: I disagree with E because I watched a documentary and the people were singing with English people and all doing the same song.
> K: I disagree with S because lots of foreign countries listen to English music 'cos that's the most common music there is and they don't make a lot of their own music in different languages.
> A: Most countries speak English. America speak a type of English.
> J: I agree with A because in different countries they learn English as well as their own language but it's actually the hardest language to learn in the world.

After some prompting from the facilitator the children returned to the original question and demonstrated pragmatic, logical and caring thinking about the merits of each visitor.

> A: I disagree and agree because the first person gave them loads of gifts like what they might need but said they were poor which was rude and selfish so the second person didn't give them anything but said let's make friends and I'll buy you what you need – could send it over to Ghana.
> T: If the first person gave them food and might never visit them again, probably run out of all the food but if the second one stayed friends with them for a long time they'd keep on helping them and giving them food.

> E: If the first one gave them food but also sat down and made friends with them, then the first one would be more help – have a friend and learn about different countries they could give more; if they didn't, then the second one would be more helpful because a friendship is more precious than something else like food.
>
> J: I disagree and agree with E because you can't have a friendship without food because you wouldn't live.

These contributions also demonstrated the children's ability to think things through and to be aware of the consequences of action or inaction. This ability to predict outcomes while evaluating the relative advantages and disadvantages of the different options suggests sophisticated thinking processes. However, these high-order thinking skills were not demonstrated by all children. Some children rarely contributed to the enquiries, but colleagues more experienced with P4C have also noted that it can take a sustained approach to enquiries, developed over terms or even a year, before some children feel ready or confident enough to contribute. What was significant was the class teacher's surprise that the quieter children, if infrequently, did share their opinions during the sessions. The teacher also commented on the rapport between the children and the facilitator, and noted that this contributed to the children feeling secure and comfortable about contributing to the discussions. The relationship that an external facilitator can establish with a class through infrequent P4C must be very different to that between a class teacher and their own class, however, perhaps there are also advantages for the class having a visitor who engages with learning in an alternative way. Areas of potential cross-curricular learning from Enquiry 4 are outlined in Figure 10.7.

Enquiry 5: Partnership and interdependence

Stimulus 5: Story about charity with artefacts.
Emerging themes: Equity, fairness, organizational issues, dual existence of wealth and poverty, diversity, creativity.

The last enquiry in the series used a story, created by the facilitator, about a brother and sister who are influenced by a television programme on the effects of poverty in an African country and resulting in them wanting to raise money for a charity. They immediately think of their aunt, who is well travelled and has worked in what they perceive to be 'poorer' countries, as they are sure she will want to donate generously. However, on sharing their idea with the aunt, she does not immediately

Enquiry 4 : Partnership and Interdependence		
Concepts: knowledge and understanding	Skills	Values and attitudes
DT: evaluate suitability of gifts **Language:** methods of communication, knowing appropriate language – I agree because … , I disagree because … **RE/PSHE:** awareness of self, and others, expectations of partnership, giving and receiving, charity, altruism, rudeness and politeness **Citizenship:** roles and responsibilities, individual's rights **Global Citizenship:** self-concept, diversity, trade not aid, interdependence	Co-operation Analysing stimulus Framing questions Evaluating questions Critical, logical, pragmatic caring thinking Voting Enquiry Speaking and listening Assume appropriate role in group Watching a role play Turn-taking Sharing opinions Responding Challenging opinions Developing arguments Reflect on own learning	Co-operative Supportive Value self and others Sense of self … I think Patience Giving constructive feedback … Respect for others' views Acceptance of different opinions Open-mindedness Mindfulness of others Empathy Showing understanding Celebrating diversity Curious Inquisitive

Figure 10.7   Areas of potential cross-curricular learning from Enquiry 4

say yes: she first shares stories about different artefacts she has brought back from South Africa, examples of the local people's creativity and resourcefulness. The aunt agrees to give the children some money for charity but asks them to think about different ways to go on supporting people in poorer countries, such as buying things they make and want to sell.

To accompany the story the artefacts that are shared by the aunt were passed around so the children could handle and evaluate them. The children listened carefully to the story and they were particularly fascinated by the artefacts. Their attention was focused on evaluating how they had been made and how well they suited their purpose. The question they chose, 'How does the story end?', provided them with opportunities to voice their opinions about the children's choices. One comment focused on the influence of the significant adult:

> I think the story should end with the children sending some money but not as much as they were going to because of the talk they were having with their aunt.
> (Year 6, July 2008)

However, they were less clear about what to do with the other half of the money, this may well have been attributable to a lack of clarity about options in the story. Most of the children's comments tended to focus on how the children would raise the money, through sponsorship or collecting, and the most efficient way to donate the money, monthly subscriptions or one-off donations. However, some children thought that linking with a specific family would ensure a personal and enduring relationship and would stimulate further curiosity about another way of life.

> I think they'll send the money and then later on in their lives maybe visit Africa.

> I think they should meet a family, send money to them yearly or visit them. (Year 6, July 2008)

Other comments reflected an understanding that Africa is a diverse continent with wealth and poverty coexisting, suggesting an understanding that the world is a complex place and that we need to be aware of assumptions we may make on the basis of limited evidence. These comments also indicate clear commitments to wealth redistribution, reallocating wealth from the richest to the poorest in order to address poverty:

> I think that J is not right, she knows that part of Africa isn't that rich but then some of Africa is rich so they should still send the amount they going to send to the poor people.

> The South Africans, the poor ones, should have half of the money that the rich Africans have; so they could all be rich instead of poor, so there could be the same amount of money in all parts of Africa. (Year 6, July 2008)

The contributions to this enquiry indicate some evidence of deeper awareness of the complexity of the issues associated with poverty. Although the children are committed to charitable responses for people in most need, there is also evidence of more challenging thinking about long-term approaches to poverty. Some of the children also indicate the value they place on knowing people and being curious about other ways of life as a way to deepen understanding and empathy, and ultimately partnership. Areas of potential cross-curricular learning from Enquiry 5 are outlined in Figure 10.8.

In conclusion

Figure 10.1 provides the overview of the project and identifies the children's developing behaviours that emerged, to different degrees, over the three terms when the P4C enquiries were run. The P4C enquiries offered children the opportunity to share their opinions about challenging and controversial issues, in a safe space, and to develop their

Enquiry 5 : Partnership and Interdependence		
Concepts: knowledge and understanding	Skills	Values and attitudes
DT: evaluate products, fit for purpose, creative designs, resourcefulness **Language:** methods of communication, knowing appropriate language – I agree because … , I disagree because … **RE/PSHE:** awareness of self, and others, expectations of partnership, giving and receiving, charity, altruism **Citizenship:** roles and responsibilities, individual's rights **Global Citizenship:** self-concept, diversity, trade not aid, interdependence **History:** compare and contrast the efficacy of objects from the present and past, **Geog:** trading partnerships, export and import **Maths:** problem-solving, investigations (trade and aid)	Co-operation Analysing stimulus Framing questions Evaluating questions Critical, logical, creative, caring thinking Voting Enquiry Speaking and listening Assume appropriate role in group Listening to a story Turn-taking Sharing opinions Responding Challenging opinions Developing arguments Planning, testing and evaluating designs and models Reflect on own learning Comparing costs Calculate Operational skills – maths	Co-operative Supportive Value self and others Sense of self … I think Patience Giving constructive feedback … Respect for other's views and rights Acceptance of different opinions Open-mindedness Mindfulness of others Empathy Showing understanding Celebrating diversity Curious Inquisitive

Figure 10.8   Areas of potential cross-curricular learning from Enquiry 5

awareness of assumptions and stereotypes and how to challenge them. The project indicated that many Year 6 children were able to engage with social justice issues through dialogue and, when provided with appropriate scaffolding, they could begin to grapple with the ethical dilemmas particularly associated with North and South community partnerships. Before the last enquiry the facilitator interviewed some of the Year 6 children from the school where most of the enquiries had taken place. Comments from the children included a considered view of the learning that had taken place during the enquiries and how it had helped develop relevant and transferable skills.

> Made to communicate with each other, say what you have to say, improved our speaking and listening. (Year 6, July 2008)

Another child's comment on how the enquiries had made her think seemed to capture a recurrent sense of awareness of social justice. This child commented on how she had liked looking at the toys and the photographs and how they had made her think 'life isn't just a breeze'. While the dilemmas – maintaining the philosophical integrity of the P4C approach, engaging children who cannot or do not want to contribute and finding time in the curriculum – remain unresolved by this project, the potential for cross-curricular learning was evident throughout the enquiries and suggests the need for further exploration and experimentation.

References

Assessment Reform Group (2002) *Assessment for Learning: 10 Principles. Research-based Principles to Guide Classroom Practice.* London: Assessment Reform Group.

Barnes, J. (2007) *Cross-curricular learning 3–14.* London: Paul Chapman Publishing.

Brand, J. (ed.) (2000) *Toying with Technology (Multimedia) A Resource for Design and Technology with a Global Perspective: Aimed at Primary 2 to 4 in Scotland, Key Stage 1 in England and Wales.* Edinburgh: Scotdec.

Dahlberg, G. and Moss, P. (2005) *Ethics and Politics in Early Childhood Education.* Oxford: RoutledgeFalmer.

Department for Education and Employment and Qualifications and Curriculum Authority (DfEE/QCA) (1999) *The National Curriculum: Handbook for Primary Teachers in England.* London: DfEE/QCA.

Department for International Development and Department for Education and Skills (DfID/DfES) (2005) *Developing the Global Dimension in the School Curriculum.* Glasgow: DfID.

Disney, A. (2003) *Citizenship and Teacher Education. Building the Professional Knowledge Base of Teacher Educators. Using School Linking as a Context for Developing Students' Understanding of Global Citizenship.* Available at WL 10.1, www.citized.info/pdf/commarticles/Anna_Disney.pdf (accessed 28 July 2008).

Fisher, R. (1998) *Teaching Thinking. Philosophical Enquiry in the Classroom.* London: Cassell.

Fisher, R. (2000) 'Philosophy for children: how philosophical enquiry can foster values education', in R. Gardner, J. Cairns and D. Lawton (eds), *Education for Values, Morals, Ethics and Citizenship in Contemporary Teaching.* London: Kogan Page.

Haynes, J. (2002) *Children as Philosophers. Learning through Enquiry and Dialogue in the Primary Classroom.* London: RoutledgeFalmer.

Hicks, D. (2007) 'Principles and precedents' in D. Hicks and C. Holden (eds), *Teaching the Global Dimension. Key Principles and Effective Practice.* London: Routledge.

Lipman, M. and Sharp, A. (1986) *Wondering at the World: Instruction Manual to Accompany 'Kio and Gus'.* London: Lanham.

Lipman, M., Sharp, A.M. and Oscanyan, F.S. (1980) *Philosophy in the Classroom.* 2nd edn. Philadelphia, PA: Temple University Press.

Open Spaces for Dialogue and Enquiry (OSDE) Available at WL 10.2, www.osdemethodology. org.uk (accessed 28 July 2008).

Oxfam (2006) *Education for Global Citizenship. A Guide for Schools.* Oxford: Oxfam.

Primary Review (2007) *Community Soundings. The Primary Review Regional Witness Sessions. Interim Report.* Cambridge: University of Cambridge.

Society for the Advancement of Philosophical Enquiry and Reflection in Education (SAPERE). Available at WL 10.3, www.sapere.org.uk/ (accessed 25 July 2008).

Smith, D.J. (2004) *If the World Were a Village.* London: A. & C. Black.

Steiner, M. (1993) *Learning from Experience. World Studies in the Primary Classroom.* Stoke-on-Trent: Trentham Books.

Young, M. and Commins, E. (2002) *Global Citizenship: The Handbook for Primary Teaching.* Cambridge: Chris Kington.

Other recommended websites

WL 10.4 Department for International Development: Global Dimension (2008), available at www.globaldimension.org.uk (accessed 25 July 2008).

WL10.5 Oxfam Education (2008), available at www.oxfam.org.uk/education (accessed 25 July 2008).

WL 10.6 Global Gateway, available at www.globalgateway.org.uk/default.aspx?page= 325 (accessed 28 July 2008).

WL 10.7 Development Education Association (DEA), available at www.dea.org.uk (accessed 28 July 2008).

WL 10.8 Global Classroom, available at http://education.guardian.co.uk/globalclassroom (accessed 28 July 2008).

Conclusion

Chris Rowley and Hilary Cooper

We began this book by wanting to provide case studies of how enquiries in the humanities could be used as the starting point for integrated work in the primary school. In addition, we wanted to show how the core values of the National Curriculum can emerge from an enquiry-led curriculum where those enquires investigate real questions in history and geography while drawing upon and developing skills learnt in other subjects.

Each chapter has, we believe, demonstrated that this can be done in quite different ways. However, a number of common factors have emerged, which seem to be needed for such enquires to be successful:

1 Collaborative planning in which different teachers bring different skills and interests. See, for example, the plans produced for the work on Chapter 6.
2 Opportunities for visiting other places which introduce new perspectives to the children. Chapters 5 and 8 both, in different ways, depend upon specific places as their stimulus.
3 Opportunities for open dialogue in which children can feel that they can contribute to the enquiry regardless of their writing skills. Chapter 10 specifically uses dialogue to develop PSHE alongside geography.
4 Clear identification of specific skills from other subjects which are rigorously developed. For example, see the way that art was developed with geography in Chapter 4.
5 An understanding of the importance of what children bring to the lesson, particularly well illustrated in Chapter 2.
6 Recognition of the importance of connections, both in the ways that our brain works and also in the connections between subjects. This is evident throughout the International School Curriculum discussed in Chapter 9.
7 Opportunities to try to 'get into the shoes' of others, whether they are from the past or from other places. Chapter 7 specifically works on this in moving children into a Tudor period.

8 Awareness of opportunities for real application of skills from other subjects. In Chapter 3 the need to apply mathematical skills becomes a
   seamless part of the theme rather than a false 'add on'.
9 Ensuring that there is a genuine enquiry into a real question, something
   that all the case studies have attempted to achieve.

These nine key factors will not, of course, be possible, or indeed desirable, in all circumstances. We believe, however, that they offer real
opportunities to develop a curriculum which is not only rigorous, but
also practical, forward looking and enriching for both children and
teachers. We hope that these case studies have inspired you to modify
and develop the ideas we have explored in your own contexts.

Index